I'm Not
Slowing
Down

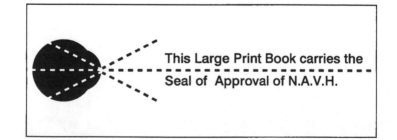

This Large Print Book carries the
Seal of Approval of N.A.V.H.

I'm Not
Slowing
Down

WINNING MY BATTLE
WITH OSTEOPOROSIS

ANN RICHARDS
with Richard U. Levine, M.D.

Thorndike Press • Waterville, Maine

Every effort has been made to ensure that the information contained in this book is complete and accurate. However, neither the author nor the publisher is engaged in rendering professional advice or services to the individual reader. The ideas, procedures, and suggestions contained in this book are not intended as a substitute for consulting with your physician. All matters regarding your health require medical supervision. Neither the author nor the publisher shall be liable or responsible for any loss, injury, or damage allegedly arising from any information or suggestion in this book.

Ann Richards is a spokesperson for Eli Lilly, which owns the patent for Evista. Dr. Richard U. Levine, M.D., has been a member of the speakers' bureau for Eli Lilly.

While the author has made every effort to provide accurate addresses, phone numbers, and Internet addresses at the time of publication, neither the publisher nor the author assumes any responsibility for errors or for changes that occur after publication.

Published in 2004 by arrangement with Dutton, a member of Penguin Group (USA) Inc.

Thorndike Press® Large Print Basic.

The tree indicium is a trademark of Thorndike Press.

The text of this Large Print edition is unabridged. Other aspects of the book may vary from the original edition.

Set in 16 pt. Plantin.

Printed in the United States on permanent paper.

Library of Congress Control Number: 2003111690
ISBN 0-7862-6067-X (lg. print : hc : alk. paper)

To my mother
— A.W.R.

As the Founder/CEO of NAVH, the only national health agency solely devoted to those who, although not totally blind, have an eye disease which could lead to serious visual impairment, I am pleased to recognize Thorndike Press* as one of the leading publishers in the large print field.

Founded in 1954 in San Francisco to prepare large print textbooks for partially seeing children, NAVH became the pioneer and standard setting agency in the preparation of large type.

Today, those publishers who meet our standards carry the prestigious "Seal of Approval" indicating high quality large print. We are delighted that Thorndike Press is one of the publishers whose titles meet these standards. We are also pleased to recognize the significant contribution Thorndike Press is making in this important and growing field.

Lorraine H. Marchi, L.H.D.
Founder/CEO
NAVH

* Thorndike Press encompasses the following imprints: Thorndike, Wheeler, Walker and Large Print Press.

CONTENTS

FOREWORD

In a report issued in 2002, the National Osteoporosis Foundation estimated that forty-four million Americans have osteoporosis or osteopenia. This number is expected to reach fifty-two million by 2010. One million bone fractures occur every year due to osteoporosis and 50,000 of these bone fractures will be hip fractures that result in death.

Detection, prevention, and treatment of osteoporosis are painless and easy. You just need to know the facts. While *I'm Not Slowing Down* was written primarily for women, since they are largely more susceptible to osteoporosis, everything in this book applies to men as well. We both share the passion to let others know how to win their battles with osteoporosis.

Our hope is that *I'm Not Slowing Down* will inspire you to be the number one advocate for your own health. Get to the gym; eat healthily; talk to your doctor. Each generation lives a little bit longer than the last. These years can be healthy, active years in which you can do whatever you want — travel, spend time with family, learn to paint. Do not let brittle bones be the reason you slow down just as life is taking off.

Ann Richards   Richard U. Levine, M.D.

A NOTE TO READERS

Ann Richards was governor of Texas from 1991 to 1995, and has been active in politics for over half a century. In 1988, she gained national prominence with her keynote address at the Democratic National Convention. She divides her time between Texas and New York City. Her personal osteoporosis regime includes a careful diet, weight-bearing and aerobic exercises, vitamins, and Evista.

Richard U. Levine, M.D., is a Clinical Professor of Obstetrics and Gynecology at the College of Physicians and Surgeons of Columbia University and Attending Physician at the New York Presbyterian Hospital, where he serves as Vice-Chairman in the department of Obstetrics and Gynecology. He has provided the medical expertise in *I'm Not Slowing Down*.

We would like to thank Rita Hamberg, Senior Director of Rehabilitation Therapies at the New York Presbyterian Hospital; Jim Karas, author of *Flip the Switch*; Ethel S. Siris, M.D., Madeline C. Stabile, Professor of Clinical Medicine, Columbia University, and Director, Toni Stabile Osteoporosis Center, New York Presbyterian Hospital.

PROLOGUE

Right after I was elected governor of Texas, we were in turmoil trying to put things together, hire staff, move into the capitol office, *and* move from my house to the Governor's Mansion. In the midst of all this, we got a notice that the Queen of England was coming to Austin. It is a real undertaking to entertain the queen. We had to go to "entertain the queen school" to learn how to act around her. Secret Service flew in from Washington to tell us where we could and could not go and what we could and could not do. On the day she was to arrive, I was in my office at the capitol when I got the call saying the queen was at the airport. I went tearing down the stairs and running across the rotunda to meet her on the capitol steps and my mother's voice went through my head as clear as a bell saying, "Where do you think you are going, to see the Queen of England?" And I thought, *Yes, Mama, I am!*

CHAPTER 1

MAMA

People do not think of osteoporosis as a fatal disease, but it is. My mother died of it. Well, that is not literally true. She died from cancer, but I swear her spirit died from osteoporosis.

Mama's name was Iona Warren, but everyone called her Ona. She was an industrious, thrifty child of the Great Depression, born and raised in a tiny town outside of Hico called Hogjaw. Her father was a farmer and they were dirt poor, but she was ambitious and hardworking — the only one of three sisters to leave home and make a life on her own. In fact, her sisters still lived in Hico when I was a child. Mama finished high school, an enormous accomplishment in her time, and left the family home to move to the big city of Waco. Today, young women do this all the time, but back then it was highly unusual and courageous. My uncle I.V. lived in

15

Waco and he encouraged Mama to come to the city. In Waco, she took a job in a dry goods store and later she met my father on a blind date.

I have told the story of the day I was born to people in the past because it perfectly illustrates her character. Before she went into labor, Mama had arranged for a neighbor lady to fix Daddy's supper on the day she delivered me, but the woman did not know how to wring a chicken's neck. To kill a chicken, you break its neck, and it takes skill to pop your arm in a way that breaks the chicken's neck clean. When my mother would do it, the head of the chicken would literally come off. That day, Mama delivered me in the morning and she was lying in bed when the neighbor came in to say she did not know how to kill the chicken. Mama said, "Bring it here," and she lay in that bed and wrung the chicken's neck.

Both my parents came from poor farming families, and all of my young life I remember Mama trying to figure out how she could make a little money, but whatever she made went for necessities or into the savings. When she was not working to make money, there were chores to be done. She spent every second housekeeping, tending the vegetable garden, sewing clothes, or taking care of our chickens.

There was no time reserved for having fun because she always had so much work to do, but she said, "You do whatever you have to do and you do it without whining." It was from Mama that I learned the value of hard work and to never linger over those things in life that could hold you back, and it had a great influence on me.

Mama taught me that you should never expect anyone else, a man included, to do what you can do for yourself. About five years before Mama died, I went to visit her and when I walked onto her patio, I looked up and saw her on the roof of the Austin condo she and my father had bought after they had sold the house in Waco. She was in her early eighties. She looked down at me and said, "I know you are going to fuss at me, but the TV said it was going to rain and the man who was supposed to clean out the gutters did not come. The periwinkles I planted the other day will be washed out if I do not clean these gutters." I just said, "Well, Mama, you have got a perfectly good reason for being on that roof and I just hope when I am your age that I can get up on a roof if I need to."

Despite her independence, my mama

began to break off in pieces. She broke her wrist, and then her arm. Mama had lost about two inches of height over the years, but no one ever mentioned the word "osteoporosis." The shrinking and broken bones were considered a natural part of aging. She was so independent that even with the cast on her arm, she refused to let me hire household help. Mama was impatient with illness. If you scratched your knee or had a stomachache, she would say, "Just get over it. I do not want to hear about that. It will be gone in the morning." Or she would say, "Go wash it off with some soap and water." It was not acceptable to feel bad because it slowed you down, and being sick was a waste of time. With each of her injuries it became harder and harder for her to keep up with the housework, but she was not going to let anybody else do it. So far as she was concerned they were not going to do it right and she would have to do it anyhow. After Daddy died and I was working in Washington, D.C., she was on her own much of the time.

I was spending half of my time in Washington, D.C., but the law firm I worked for had an office in Austin, so I would commute from D.C. to Austin every week or so to make sure she was doing okay.

As the years went by, there were a few warning signs that Mama was not well. She would lose her train of thought in the middle of a sentence. She got lost driving from her house to my house. Her driving scared the family to no end! When she fell and broke her arm, she had to stop driving and we took her car one day and disabled it so that she could not drive. We kept telling her we would get it fixed, but of course we were not going to do it. Then one day, my son Clark and his wife, Sharon, were sitting at the kitchen table with Mama when she fainted. They took her to the hospital, and it was then that we learned my mother had a malignant lesion on her brain.

Mama was sent for radiation treatment. She was sick and lost her hair, but she would not wear a wig, so I bought scarves and hats for her. When I gave them to her, though, she would say, "Why did you spend your money on that?" Or I would take her to the hospital and when we arrived she would say, "I know how busy you are so do not bother coming in with me." That was her way. She did not want to be an inconvenience and I understand it because I worry that I will end up an inconvenience to my children.

Not long after she was diagnosed with cancer, she left something burning on the stove in her condominium. And though I did not want to relocate her on top of everything else, I knew there was no way she could continue to live alone. I really admire the Chinese and the Mexican cultures for how they take care of their elders by bringing them into the family, but there was no way I could make a living and give Mama the care she needed. Besides, my mother cherished her own space and she would have hated living under my roof. It is funny how much like my mother I become as I get older, and how, like her, I often crave solitude. I suppose we get set in our ways, used to our own spaces, our own ways of doing things, but I still needed to figure out something that would make Mama comfortable. I asked Mama if she would allow me to take a look at an assisted-living apartment for her and she said yes, she thought she would, and she said that she was just as concerned about her ability to care for herself as I was.

After considering a few options, we found an assisted-living facility in Austin that combined three sections: go-go, slow-go, and no-go. I wanted a place that would allow her to remain in the same facility; moving is so disorienting. The rules of the facility required Mama to be able to take care of herself when we first bought the apartment. This is called the "go-go" stage because she could still care for herself. If we waited until she could no longer care for herself, it would be too late to get her into that particular facility. Once we bought the apartment, it would be Mama's for the rest of her life, and if she needed assistance it was available in the slow-go or no-go sections. When she died, the go-go apartment would be sold to someone else.

Not long after our discussion, we moved Mama into her new assisted-living apartment. What a job! Years and years of accumulated stuff — my mother saved everything. By the end of her life, she had clothes hanging in her closet she had not worn in years. She was certain that one day she would need that old sequin dress! It had reached the point where there was no more room in the closet and she had started hanging things on a rod over the bathtub. The garage was filled with boxes full of paper bags from the grocery store and plastic sacks full of more plastic sacks. She never threw away a ragged towel or old socks since these could be used for cleaning. Before my father died I had arranged for Meals on Wheels to help out, and when I came to visit, I would find the refrigerator filled with leftover Meals on Wheels boxes. If they did not eat everything in the box, Mama would save what was left. Even after she was on her own, she saved her leftovers. The problem was, she could not remember what was in the cartons — it was just a mess. And because Mama was a gardener there were always boxes and sacks of dirt in the garage. She was big on bringing dirt home. She would see some dirt on the side of the road that looked rich, stop, get the shovel out of the trunk, and fill up a box. When we moved her things out of the condo, she loaded a box of dirt into the car trunk because she said she would need dirt for potting plants. She had antique china dolls with elaborate dresses, and there were china cabinets full of cut glass and figurines. We found multiple lists: "silver service in hot water-heater closet, Indian jewelry under stairs." Time had dulled her memory so she had to make lists, but then she could not remember where she'd put the lists. Mama spent a lifetime worrying that I would not appreciate the things she collected, but the truth is that toward the end she lost interest in all that stuff herself. All that mattered to her were family and friends; everything else sort of fell away. All she cared about was having us visit. Life was measured from visit to visit.

Mama's new apartment was really quite pretty. It was important that she have the option to prepare her own meals or choose to go to the central dining room because I wanted to be certain that she could remain independent for as long as possible. At first, Mama was adjusting well and I think having other people around gave her back some of her confidence, but then she fell and broke her hip. I do not know how long she lay on the floor before someone found her. Now, for anyone to experience an accident is difficult, but for older people, it is traumatic. There are so many different stages of treatment that require different facilities, different doctors, and multiple medications. They lose track of where they are and for what reason. They go to the emergency room and there is one set of doctors and nurses. Then, from the emergency room they are moved to a regular hospital room and there is another set of doctors and nurses. If they need to have a bone set or have surgery, there is another specialist and a new group of nurses. Once past that, they are moved to a rehab center, where there is a new group of therapists, nurses, and physicians. For those who leave the rehab but are not well enough to go home, there is a way-station facility and another set of personnel. And then by the time they get home, *if* they get home, there is a home-health care nurse and a rehab therapist. And on top of all this confusion, they have to decipher the label on the medicine bottles that instructs them on what to take, how much, and when. It is no wonder my mama became terribly confused when she broke her hip.

When Mama got out of rehab, she was unsteady on her feet and could not return to her go-go apartment, so while she recovered, she stayed in the slow-go section of the assisted-living facility. We all wanted what was best for her, but looking back, I think moving around like that caused Mama a great deal of confusion. Even in the go-go apartment that was furnished with her things, she sometimes became puzzled about where she was. When she left the central dining room, she would get lost looking for her apartment. As Mama was shuffled around from one place to another after her accident, her confusion escalated. When she was in the rehabilitation unit, the doctor would question her and Mama would answer, "Well yes and thank you" — always very courteous — but after he left the room she would say, "Who was that?" And I would say, "Well, that is the doctor here in the rehab center." "Oh," she would say with resignation.

Mama had to use a walker and she hated it. Now began a real, real serious loss of cognizance, and this time in her life is a very painful memory for me. We visited her a lot, but she would forget anyone had been there and the very next day after one of us had been there, she would ask why we never came to see her. She would call me or my daughters and say, "I am at a hotel downtown. I need somebody to pick me up." I put some of the furniture from her go-go apartment into the slow-go room so she would see familiar things. When she would call me in confusion, I would try to talk her through it. I would say, "Mama, you see those chairs there? You remember we got those chairs covered in that new fabric?" And she would say, "Yes." "So you know that those are your chairs and you are in your room." And she would say, "Well, I guess I am." Once I went into her room and found she had written "help me" in lipstick on the mirror in the bathroom.

My heart broke when I read her message. I just know that she got up in the middle of the night and did not know where she was.

I thank God for the slow-go nursing-care unit in the assisted-living complex because I never would have wanted to move her to yet another location. The facility was really nice, but I had a sinking feeling of sadness every time I walked out the door and left her there. Except for the delusional periods, Mama was not afraid. She did not talk much in those last months, but she wanted us to talk to her. We talked about the weather, what the weather was yesterday, what the weather would be tomorrow, what the children were doing, and what the grandchildren were thinking. Mama did not complain, and she would not have wanted us to complain on her behalf, but she did not have any control over her situation or an opportunity to alter her circumstances. For a woman with Mama's spunk, I sometimes think it might have been worse than dying.

We would take her out for Sunday brunch and that really cheered her up. We would go to Luby's, where she could get her favorite vegetables, and she would tell me that some of the people in the nursing home were really crazy! There was a woman who shouted all the time and a man who never talked at all. The complex had a minister come once a week, and she would attend even though she said he was boring. And a church lady came and sang songs that Mama enjoyed. I remember her seated in a circle with a group of other women. They were rolling a red ball back and forth to each other, a form of exercise I suppose. Even with the walker that she hated, Mama tried to participate in life until the end, but it was obvious that she was dying. I was still commuting between Austin and Washington, D.C., and I was giving speeches all over the country, so I hired someone to stay with Mama all the time, and we got hospice care.

My mother told me at some point in those last few weeks that she had seen her mother, although in reality she had been dead for many years. My mother loved her own mother dearly. She said that my grandmother had come to her room and sat with her.

In the last days of her life, hospice caregivers told us that even though Mama was in a coma, she might still hear and understand what we said to her. The night my mother died I talked to her. I said, "Do you know how you told me you saw your

Mama? Maybe you are really going to get to see her." I said, "You know, Mama, I do not know what heaven is like, but if it is there, then Daddy will be there and Grandmother and Aunt Elta. You will get to be with them." My children talked to her, too. Whether that was any reassurance to her or not I do not know, but I like to think it was.

I have come to the conclusion that not only do we have to learn to live well during the years we have, but we also have to learn to accept dying. We should be allowed to live out our last days with dignity. Mama had signed the power of attorney and the power of medical decisions and every necessary document because she did not want to die an ignoble death, but her death was hard. She went through all of the sad, gasping death throes. I keep thinking that as time passes, that memory will fade, but it has not. In her last days, Mama was not conscious. She had to be turned to avoid bedsores. The day before she died, I came into her room to find one of the staff members at the nursing home spooning a black substance into her mouth. Mama was semiconscious and unable to swallow because her mouth was so ulcerated. I was shocked and upset so I said, "What are you doing?" And the woman replied, "I am giving her vitamins." I could not believe it — Mama was dying, but since the doctor had not marked "vitamins" off the chart, the woman had mashed vitamins into chocolate pudding and attempted to administer the stuff even though my mother could not swallow.

I did not realize how strong our bodies are until I watched my mother die. Dying is hard. Shepherding her through those last years was traumatic. The last lesson I learned from my mama was to put my health first. I do not want my kids to remember my last years the way I remember Mama's.

Mama died on February 15, 1997, just after midnight of Valentine's Day. For a long time I felt untethered from the world, like a balloon whose string is suddenly severed.

I often think about what I should have done or could have done when she was dying. I think that I did all I could. It is just that she was failing more rapidly than any of us were willing to accept. I do not think most of us want to admit that our mother is dying. I kept thinking that with every illness, she was going to spring back, because she always had. I would not have wanted her to live one minute longer the way that she was. That is no life. When I think about this sad time, I realize the real regret I have about my mother is that she had to move into assisted living. Not long ago I bought a new condo. It has a spare bedroom I call the nurse's room, and I intend to make the place easy for me to negotiate in my old age. I want to live as long as possible in my own home.

After Mama died, I talked a lot about my mother's aging and dying in speeches I made around the country. I talked about how we have to take responsibility for our own health. We can give no greater gift to those we love than our good health. I tapped into something with those speeches. Women came up to me afterward and talked about their own fears of aging and remaining independent. They talked about their situation with their own aging parents and I realized that there is little shared information about our feelings when our parents need care.

I do not know why I have such a fear that my children might have to be responsible for me when I am old, but I do. I hope I am still doing the same thing I am doing now when I am eighty, but I may not, so I need money in the bank that can support my needs and will let me travel, and indulge my children. I do not want to be limited by the lack of money or by my physical health. These are the two things that women think the least about when they are young. Women are always caring for somebody else. I do not know why it is that way, but it has always been that way.

Mama held on to her gumption for a long time, but her body and mind had given up. If I had known then what I know now about osteoporosis, years before my mama had broken that first bone, I would have insisted she get a bone-density test and from there, choose a regimen to strengthen her bones. It would not have kept her from dying, but her last years would have been better. Watching Mama, I knew I was seeing myself in a few years, and it motivated me to become aggressive about taking care of myself.

Osteoporosis makes living difficult and that is why it is so frightening. The good news though is that new medical information and medications offer women the opportunity to overcome this disease. What matters to me is being independent for the rest of my life, able to do whatever I want without being held back by infirmities. I do not want to end up in a trailer in my daughter's driveway. I have tried to lead an active, productive life, but I did not always take care of my health. I want to keep doing the things I enjoy; so today I make my health my top concern.

CHAPTER 2

FAMILY

I was born in my parents' bedroom in a little community called Lakeview. We lived in a little country house, with a swing on the porch and a white fence in front. I got all the benefits and deficits of being an only child. Although we were not well off, I never wanted for anything. I was expected to do my part around the house, and Mama was strict about that — you never went anywhere until the animals had been fed and the garden watered. Even then, I was not allowed to play away from the house for more than one hour at a time, and if I did not come home, my mother would come and get me.

There was not a whole lot to do in Lakeview. One year Mama signed me up for "Expression." For fifty cents, a woman would teach us to recite children's poems and once or twice a year, we had a recital where I would get a chance to show my skill in performing. Those expression lessons are part of the reason that I never had a fear of public speaking. I was always assertive, but the expression classes gave me poise and self-assurance in front of an audience.

My father's name was Cecil Willis. I named my firstborn, Cecile, after him. He was a great raconteur and by that I do not mean he just told great stories; he told great dirty jokes. Daddy thought I was the best thing that ever happened to him and he took me everywhere. He would show me off where he worked at Southwestern Drug. He was very proud of me and it was his love and support that gave me the self-confidence to do the things that I have done in my life. Thanks to him, I was in college before I found out I was not the smartest thing on the planet.

During World War II, my father was drafted and he joined the Navy. After a few months, my mother decided we should move to San Diego, where he was stationed. In those days, women did not just hop into their cars with children and drive cross-country, but you could not tell that to my mother. She filled the car with provisions and we were on our way. We took along Mama's second cousin, Fannabee

Fryer, to help with the driving.

It took a long time and it was *sooo* hot. In those days cars were not air-conditioned. I did not think it could get hotter than Texas, but it was terrible driving across the desert. I do not know where we slept because my mother would not have spent the money to sleep in a hotel, and motels were not that common.

When we arrived, we had to live in a basement room of someone's house until we found an apartment. That apartment was so small I had to get up and fold my sleeping cot every morning so my father could get through the living room. I guess for that reason, it was good that he was home only on weekends.

My mother was a skilled seamstress. We put a sign in the window that said ALTERATIONS AND DRESSMAKING. While she was not flooded with customers, she earned enough extra money to pay the bills. I was in the eighth grade. I went to Theodore Roosevelt Junior High, which was so far across town that I had to take a bus to a streetcar that would take me there. To me, San Diego was exotic. For the first time, I attended school with kids from different backgrounds. There was Helen Castenada, Josephine Giacalone. There were African-American kids, Italian kids, Greek, and Hispanic. Living in San Diego opened my eyes. After that, I could never understand racial prejudice.

While we were in San Diego, my mother had an ectopic pregnancy and she was quite ill. Some of the wives of the men my father had met in the service lived in San Diego, so there were people to help take care of her. In fact, just the other day I got a call from someone who wanted to know if I was the Dorothy Ann Willis she had been looking for. Her aunt was someone we had known in San Diego and, of course, she is quite elderly now, but her niece wanted to put us together, to touch base.

After the war, we came home to Texas. We sold the house in Lakeview and moved into town so that I could go to Waco High School. Everyone knows me by Ann, but my first name is really Dorothy. I was named for two women who worked with my father at Southwestern Drug. I guess my parents just liked the names, but I dropped the Dorothy when I went to Waco High School. During World War II, there was a popular saying, "dot, dot, dash." It was Morse Code for the letter V, short for "victory." It is what the navy ships would signal to each other, and it became part of the lexicon. Kids would tease me saying "dot, dot, dash" and I just hated it, so when I registered for high school I told them my name was Ann. When I came home, my parents were stunned that I had a new name, but they got over it.

In Waco, my parents bought a parcel of land on North 35th Street and Daddy went back to Southwestern Drug while Mama built us a house. She drew up the blueprints with a friend who was a builder and each day she drove down to pick up day workers. She straw-bossed the day laborers and managed to build a substantial house. It had two bedrooms, a den with a fireplace, a living room with another fireplace, and big picture windows. There was a room called a "breezeway" that led from the house to a two-car garage. The exterior was Austin stone and there was a big cement patio in back with a barbecue pit. My mother found antique mantels, brass doorknobs, doorplates, and other accoutrements from an old house being demolished. I spent hours cleaning those brass fixtures, but they were beautiful. My mother loved that house — and for good reason. It was a real testimony to her ability and ingenuity.

My mother gave me the grit to work hard, but my father gave me self-confidence. When I was fourteen, I learned to drive his car. It was an Oldsmobile and because his legs were so long, the car he drove had the seat pushed way back. I could not adjust the seat because it was broken, so I learned to drive with the gas pedal too far away. I was all scrunched down in the seat so I could reach the pedals. We must have been a sight! My father so tall in the seat he nearly hit the roof, and me barely able to see over the steering wheel. For years, I was unable to drive a car unless the seat was pushed all the way back.

I was on the debate team in high school and ultimately I went to Baylor University on a debating scholarship. When I came home after winning a tournament, Mama would not say she was proud of me because that was not her way. Instead she would cook fried chicken and macaroni and cheese for dinner. That was how she let me know that she was proud of me.

Like a lot of parents, my mother wanted *her* dreams to be fulfilled in me. I felt that responsibility. I think my mother hoped I would have a life of leisure and great creature comforts. I do not think she ever imagined that I would get involved in politics and public life. If there is such a thing as a professional housewife, thanks to my mama, that is what I was trained to do. And I was good at it.

I met David Richards in Waco High School. David had a background that I did not have; his parents were both college graduates and were a part of the affluent set of Waco. He was handsome and dark, while I was blond and blue eyed. We loved each other as much as two young people can and soon, despite some parental intervention, we were inseparable. We married in 1953. I was nineteen.

David started college at the University of Texas at Austin, but he transferred to be with me at Baylor. When we graduated, David went on to law school at the University of Texas, and then we moved to Dallas and had our first baby, Cecile. When Cecile was born, my parents were overjoyed. Not quite two years later, our second child, Dan, was born. After Dallas there was Washington, D.C., where David worked as an attorney on the Civil Rights Commission and we rented a house on Capitol Hill. I would leave Cecile and Dan with a baby-sitter once a week so I could sit in the Senate to hear the debates. Ironically, the politics in Washington, D.C., were not as interesting or as productive as those we were involved with in Texas, so we headed home. Clark, our third child, was born soon after. I helped form the North Dallas Democratic Women's Club and worked as a volunteer in a lot of political campaigns. Our fourth child, Ellen, was born in Dallas.

My parents were wonderful to my children. Each summer Cecile, Dan, Clark, and Ellen would visit them and they had a grand time. Mama taught the girls to sew and Daddy taught the boys to fish. As youngsters, Cecile, Dan, Clark, and Ellen were involved in everything we did. In 1969 we moved to the Austin hill country. We bought an old house on Red Bud Trail in Westlake Hills. The minute I saw the house, I knew it was where we had to live. It was one story, limestone, with the original hardwood floors, but the best thing about the house was that it was built overlooking the cleft of a canyon. I built an addition to the house that included a big living room and a screened-in porch that framed a great view of downtown Austin. My son Clark said that Austin looked like a "garden of lights."

My family had fabulous Christmas celebrations in that house. Christmas Eve was always a big party. All four grandparents would come for the holiday and our neighbors would bring their kids. The living room ceilings were high and we would get the tallest tree we could find, ten feet or more. I had collected ornaments over the years so not a single ornament on the tree was alike. Years earlier, I had made a train for the kids with coffee can lids for wheels and shiny wrapping paper over boxes for the cars and we put that on the bookcase with a fat, stuffed Santa in front. Somewhere we had found lots of cloth elves that we would perch about on the train cars. We would sing carols and act out *The Twelve Days of Christmas.* When I moved into the Governor's Mansion, my children were grown and my marriage had ended after thirty years, but we brought that Christmas Eve tradition with us.

In the seventies, a group of us decided that issues of concern to women needed to be addressed, and that opportunities for women needed promotion. So together, we began the Texas Foundation for Women's Resources. I was on the initial board along with Jane Hickie, Sarah Weddington, Judith Guthrie, Martha Smiley, and Cathy Bonner. Mary Beth Rogers and Ruthe

Winegarten joined our efforts to coordinate an exhibit on women in Texas history. The Texas Foundation for Women's Resources also works to provide a support system and network for mentoring women. Through them, foundation programs like Leadership Texas, Leadership America, and the Power Pipeline got their start. Books for schools have been published with help from the foundation and money was raised by the foundation, so that women could be included in *The Handbook of Texas*, the definitive history of Texas. In Dallas, we recently opened the first museum in the world devoted to women, The Women's Museum: An Institute for the Future.

These women who served on that initial board, along with my friend, Claire Korioth, are remarkable. They are my support system and they were the core of my political team. They helped shape the objectives, the ideals, and goals I set for myself today. I feel so fortunate to have these women as friends.

When I ran for public office the first time, in 1976, my husband actually had been asked to run and chose not to do so. A group of my friends then turned to me. I had been active in the women's movement for years. Now it was time for me to put up or shut up. In 1976, I was elected Travis County Commissioner.

When I ran for state treasurer, my son, Dan, traveled with me for nine months as I campaigned across Texas. He was also with me on the campaign trail when I first ran for governor. He was an enormous help to me. Crowds get larger and more intense as the campaign continues. Toward the end, the press travels with you and they swarm around you everywhere you go. You are "on" from six in the morning until ten at night. Dan was like a trainer during a heavyweight championship boxing fight. I could slump in my corner when the closing bell rang and he would slap my shoulders, make sure the cut man fixed my face, and he would get me back into the ring no matter what. And who can you let your guard down around if not your son? Dan has always been very protective of me and when difficulties arose, he was right there. In 1982, I was voted in as Treasurer of the State of Texas. I was the first woman elected to statewide office in Texas in fifty years.

My daughter Cecile, and my son-in-law Kirk Adams, moved to Texas for the first gubernatorial race.

By 1989, the year I was campaigning for

governor of Texas, my father had begun to lose his eyesight from macular degeneration. He could no longer drive a car and it was hard for him to do much, but that did not stop him from campaigning for me. Someone would take him up the courthouse steps of whatever town we were in and he would hand out campaign literature. Or, Mama would drive him around and he would put up posters. He would get so furious about the negative campaign ads my opponents would run that he would argue out loud with the TV.

Through everything, he was in my corner. I remember how nervous I was to tell my parents I was going to get a divorce. I had been married such a long time that I knew it would upset them. I drove up to Waco filled with dread and when I got there, Daddy and I went out to see the garden. It was summer and the garden was filled with squash and tomatoes. After a moment, I said, "Daddy, I really need to talk with you because I am going to get a divorce." I expected him to tell me to think about it some more and what a sad thing it would be, but he did not miss a beat. He said, "Take my advice. If it is not good for you, get out of it." I was truly taken aback. My parents' marriage was not idyllic, but they had stayed together through thick and thin. I know my mother loved my father very much, but she was demanding. At the end of his life, I think my father's blindness was frustrating for her. In his last years, he could not watch TV and he could not read. We got a tape player and tapes for him, but eventually he could not operate the recorder. He would get the tape started and something would happen so that the tape would cut off and he could not fix it. Mama wanted to do things, but when he lost his sight she had to care for him instead. It is difficult to watch your parents go through something like that. You do not want to choose sides, but I am not sure I was as sympathetic as I could have been with my mother.

Along with the blindness, my father shrank four inches or so in his later years. He was stooped and walked with a cane, his head pushed forward. We never think of men getting osteoporosis, but they do, and while my father did not break any bones, he must have had hairline fractures in his spine to be so stooped.

In 1990, I was elected the forty-fifth governor of the state of Texas. I loved being governor. Despite the frustrations and the disappointments — which are many —

there is no work more rewarding than public service. Back in 1992, I was on a ranch in West Texas, where I was waiting for my ride back to the place I was staying. I was left alone for a few minutes (an uncommon occurrence back then) and while I was standing there, the ranch foreman hesitantly ambled up to me and asked for an autograph. He was an older man, probably in his seventies. From his manner, I could tell he was the real thing — a Texan who had put his life and heart into the land and never strayed far from what was literally home on the range. He stood there sort of shy and courtly and held out what we used to call a "nickel spiral notebook" for my signature. While I was writing, he said, "I cannot even imagine what a great honor it must be to be the governor of Texas." When I looked up at him, he had just a hint of tears brimming in his eyes. I cannot begin to explain how deeply that touched me, and the experience pulled me up short. He was right, of course. It was a great honor. After all, when my grandmother was a girl, according to Texas law, the only people who could not vote were "idiots, imbeciles, the insane, and women." Less than one lifetime later, I was the governor of Texas.

Being governor was a full-time job — one that I worked hard to get and worked hard every day to do. The showcase of being governor can be arresting — from inside as well as out. When the Queen of England, Elizabeth II, came to visit Texas with Prince Philip, she gave a wonderful dinner upon the conclusion of her trip. As we were standing in the receiving line, the mayors of Texas cities started coming through — Houston, Dallas, San Antonio, San Marcos, Corpus Christi, Galveston — and they were all women. Prince Philip turned to me and said, "I say, it looks as though this state is rather like a matriarchy." And, without so much as a pause, the Queen said, "I think that is very nice, don't you?" It was a great line, but matriarchy is not what we are after. We have learned that when the scales are weighted in favor of one gender or one race or one privileged background, no one is well served. The truth is that we cannot solve any of our problems until our institutions — both private and public — reflect the diversity of our population. So, if I had to choose one thing I accomplished as governor, it would be that I changed the face of state government in Texas by appointing minorities and women. I have felt that government often leaves out the people it serves. In the establishment of government policies those policies should be made by including individuals affected by them. It is not that one gender or race is better than another, but rather that we bring different perspectives to problems because of our different experiences. The most sympathetic and sensitive of our men friends, no matter how hard they try, cannot hear with a woman's ear or process information through a woman's experience. Hispanics and African-Americans have patiently — and usually with uncommon gentleness — tried to explain to Anglos for years that issues are seen differently from inside a brown or black skin.

A debate about funding for mental retardation facilities is changed tremendously by the presence of a parent of a child with Down's syndrome.

A dialogue about equal opportunity takes new meaning and immediacy when a person of color is in the room.

The analogies are endless, but the point is always the same. When you add someone whose understanding is instinctive and not just intellectual, the whole equation changes. Because our backgrounds are different, we pick up different nuances and bring valuable skills to the decision-making process.

In the first gubernatorial campaign against Clayton Williams, Cecile was pregnant with twins and she sat at her desk in the campaign office with a fetal monitor strapped across her belly. My relationship with my children is precious, and their friendship means more to me than I know how to express. It is hard to be your kids' friend. I will always be their mother, but to have them want to spend time with me is a rare gift. I believe that part of the reason my relationship with my children is so special is that I am too busy to tell them what I think they ought to do. I recognize the kind of person I am — not only do I run my life, but I can get into the business of running everyone else's life, too.

When I speak to women about raising children, I say the benefit to young children of a stay-at-home mother is over-rated. The right-wingers tell poor women that the country went to hell because they stay home with their kids instead of going to work. And then they tell middle-class women that the country went to hell because they want to work instead of staying home with their kids. Not since Adam said

"Eve made me do it" have women taken the rap for so many problems.

When people ask me how I felt about losing to George Bush in '94, I tell them I mourned for three seconds and got over it. Mama taught me not to cry over spilt milk.

By 1994, Daddy had not felt well for a long time, but my father was part of a family that did not complain. One day, I was at their condo and it was clear to me that he was in pain. I took him to the doctor, but he could not find anything wrong with him. Later that night, we had to take him to the hospital because he was in so much pain. After a series of tests, they discovered he had esophageal cancer. He was put on a morphine drip and I think he was unconscious from that point on. The following night, my father died.

Driving back from the hospital with the seat pushed way back, I thought about all that he had done for me and I still tear up when I see a photograph of him.

In 1995, I got a job in Washington, D.C., lobbying for a law firm, Verner, Liipfert, Bernhard, McPherson & Hand. Now, I work for Public Strategies, Inc., with my good friend Jack Martin in Austin and New York, which makes me incredibly happy because I love both cities.

CHAPTER 3

GETTING A BONE-DENSITY TEST

In 1996, I was working in D.C. and commuting to Austin. By now Mama was really ill and so her health was on my mind every day. It is funny how often it is not one big thing that finally captures our attention, but a series of things or a chain of events. That year, a few things started to occur that made me wonder about my own health. First, my collars did not seem to fit right anymore. My mother taught me to sew and she was very particular about how things fit — whether the stripes matched at the seams and so on. Tailoring was important to her so, of course, tailoring was important to me as well. In 1996, I began to notice that when I sat down my shirt collar or my coat collar would rise up to my hairline in the back. It was strange because my collars had always laid flat on my neck and shoulders. I could not figure it out. One afternoon, as I was sitting there with my collar creeping up my neck, I realized I might be shrinking. Something clicked and I remembered my mother breaking bones, my father stooped, and his mother, Nanny, with her broken arm and bent back.

Our parents are like a crystal ball. I believe that just by looking at them, you can predict your own health and how you will look later in life. In addition to my parents, my grandmothers both had osteoporosis. I used to spend a lot of time with Nanny when I was a child. I would take my doll and go to her house, where she would make doll clothes out of scraps of fabric, lace, and ribbons. Nanny was so bent over that I do not remember her any other way. When I was a child, I wondered if Nanny's bowed back had anything to do with bending over the sewing machine. My mother's mother was small and always stood erect, but as she aged she became shorter.

Right about this time, it occurred to me that I might be shrinking like my parents and grandparents had. My daughter Ellen and I were walking around Town Lake and I tripped on some gravel and lost my footing. I put my hand down to break my fall and I broke two bones in my left hand. It hurt terribly! Because the break was so bad, I had to have surgery to repair it. I had all sorts of metal screws and pins sticking out of my hand. It looked like the Frankenstein monster's hand. I was in a cast for what seemed like forever. Once they removed the cast, my hand was in a brace and the pins were still in place.

I was determined that I was not going to let my broken hand slow me down. I tried to do everything I always did, but while I had that cast and those pins, life was not the same. They got in the way of everything I tried to do, and it is a good thing I am right handed or I would have really been constrained by not being able to write.

After watching my mother's struggle, my creeping collars, and the broken hand, I went to my doctor for my annual physical and I asked for a bone-density test. The result was that I was diagnosed with osteopenia, the early stages of osteoporosis.

I have been seeing the same doctor for a long time and I respect him very much. I know he reads the current journals and stays abreast of new medical discoveries, but I also know he has hundreds of other patients. Doctors are not shamans. They are human beings and they might not always remember every detail in a medical record. My doctor always told me if I had a question, then I should ask. Any doctor should be happy to answer questions about health. That is what he or she is there to do, but everyone must become an advocate for their own health. Many doctors are overworked and medicine has become increasingly more specialized. General practitioners often refer patients to specialists. Despite the fact that records are transferred, one doctor might not know what the other is doing. It is crucial to good care that the patient provide information about his or her treatment.

Bone-density testing (densitometry) is the vehicle that has revolutionized the diagnosis and treatment of osteoporosis. It gives doctors the opportunity to identify a woman at risk before she has broken a bone so she can be put on medication, as well as start an exercise and diet program which will strengthen her bones.

Bone density is a measure of how much bone mineral is found within the bone. Most devices use the metric system, so density is measured in grams per square centimeter (g/cm^2) or grams per cubic centimeter (g/cc). Unlike an X ray, most of the test information comes not from the pictures of the bones, but from the density numbers. However, some machines take an additional picture of the whole spine to look for undiagnosed fractures. Once bone density is measured, it is compared to that of an average young adult (T-score) and to the average of an individual of the same age (z-score).

In 1994, The World Health Organization (WHO) published guidelines establishing "average" measurements, known as T-scores. This is the criterion used by most physicians today. One important point: The World Health Organization restricted these criteria to measurements made in postmenopausal woman only. A box of The World Health Organization T-scores appears on page 64.

Most women do not get a bone-density test until they are experiencing menopause. They see the doctor because they want relief from hot flashes and other symptoms of menopause. It is at this point that the doctor might suggest a bone-density test. Waiting until many years past menopause can be unfortunate because a woman can lose 30 percent of her bone density in the first five years after menopause!

In 1997, Congress passed the Bone Mass Measurement Act. This legislation outlines who is eligible for Medicare reimbursement for a bone-density measurement. Private insurers tend to follow Medicare's lead, but some states, such as Texas, passed legislation that mandated private insurers to offer coverage.

Here is who is eligible for Medicare reimbursement under the Bone Mass Measurement Act:

- An estrogen-deficient woman at clinical risk for osteoporosis as determined by her physician or a qualified nonphysician practitioner who is treating her

- An individual with vertebral abnormalities on an X ray that suggest osteoporosis, osteopenia, or a fracture

- An individual who is receiving or who expects to receive steroid therapy equivalent to 7.5mg of prednisone (or greater per day) for three months

- An individual with primary hyperparathyroidism

- An individual who is being monitored

to determine the response to effectiveness of a therapy for osteoporosis that has been approved by the Food and Drug Administration

The Bone Mass Measurement Act stipulates that the test is reimbursable every twenty-three months under these guidelines.

Despite the criteria set for Medicare payments, I think that every woman should have a bone-density test, ideally at menopause. Knowing my bone density has helped me make decisions about a regimen to prevent osteoporosis. The National Osteoporosis Foundation's recommendations for who should have a bone-density test are somewhat different than the criteria set for Medicare.

The National Osteoporosis Foundation recommends the following have a bone-density measurement taken (Note: these guidelines are for postmenopausal women only):

- All women age 65 or over

- Postmenopausal women under the age of 65 who have one or more risk factors for osteoporosis

- Postmenopausal women who have a fracture

- Women who have been taking ERT or HRT for prolonged periods

- Women who are considering therapy for osteoporosis when knowledge of the bone density would aid in that decision.

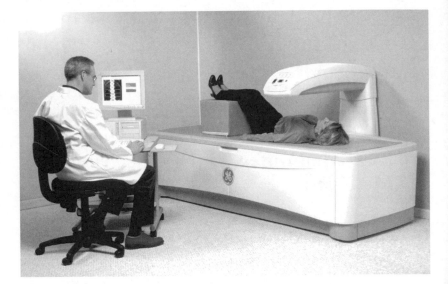

3.1

The Lunar Prodigy, a central DEXA bone densitometer, manufactured of GE Medical Systems, Madison, WI.
PHOTO REPRODUCED WITH PERMISSION OF GE MEDICAL SYSTEMS, MADISON, WI.

There are a few different bone-density test devices, but the test itself is easy and painless. For my test, I lay on a flat, padded table with my feet propped up on a foam block. I was able to keep my clothes on since I did not have on any metal or dense plastic. For the hipbone test, my feet had to be flat, so a positioning device was used to hold my feet at the proper angle. The scanning for a complete spine and hip test was less than a minute each.

My Bone-Density Test 5/17/2002

Figure 3.2 is a close-up image of my spine. The vertebrae are outlined. The horizontal lines go through the disk spaces. Each vertebra is labeled to the left of the image. T12 indicates the twelfth thoracic vertebra. The lumbar vertebrae are labeled L1, L2, and so on. My ribs can be seen projecting down from the thoracic vertebra at the top of the image, and the pelvis can be seen on either side of the spine at the bottom of the photo.

The technologist and physician use this photo to make sure that the bones are labeled properly. Instead of using just one vertebra to diagnose osteoporosis or predict fracture risk, the average bone density of at least three or four spine bones will be used.

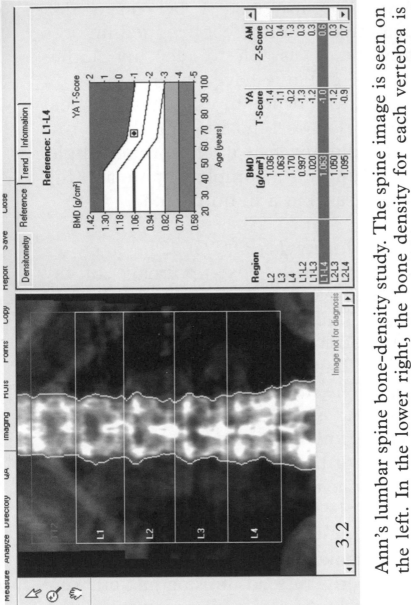

Ann's lumbar spine bone-density study. The spine image is seen on the left. In the lower right, the bone density for each vertebra is listed as well as the average bone density for every combination of vertebrae.

A hip fracture is a fracture of the upper portion of the femur. This fracture is potentially the most devastating, possibly resulting in a loss of physical independence and even death.

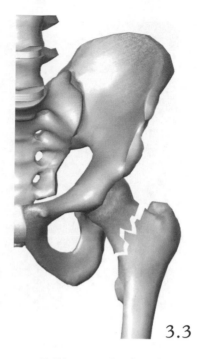

3.3

When my L1–L4 Bone Mineral Density (BMD) is compared to the average for a young woman, it is 90 percent of the predicted value. Compared to other women my age and weight it is 107 percent. This means that while I am 10 percent below the average value for a young adult, I am 7 percent better than one would have predicted for my age. My goal is to have a *better* number than (not even with) what is predicted for my age because women are expected to lose bone as they get older. Of course, this recent bone-density test was taken after I had been lifting weights and taking osteoporosis prevention medication for four years.

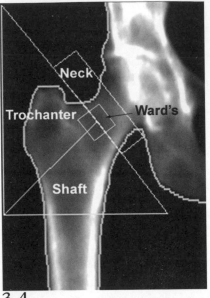

The hip as seen during a DEXA hipbone density study. This is really the upper, or proximal, portion of the femur. It is divided into the four areas seen in the image. The neck, trochanter, and shaft are also combined to make the "total" region.

3.4

My hip image is shown in Figure 3.4. Calling this a hipbone-density study is incorrect. There really is no such thing as the "hipbone." There is a joint. When someone is said to have "broken a hip," the bone that actually breaks is the upper part of the femur. When doctors do a "hipbone density" this is the area they are measuring.

Figure 3.4 is a detailed image of my left hipbone-density study. Although doctors are interested in only the "proximal" femur, the figure is divided into four areas: neck, Ward's area, trochanter, and shaft. Ward's area and the shaft are really not particularly useful to this test. The femoral neck and the trochanter are of great interest because here is where fractures occur.

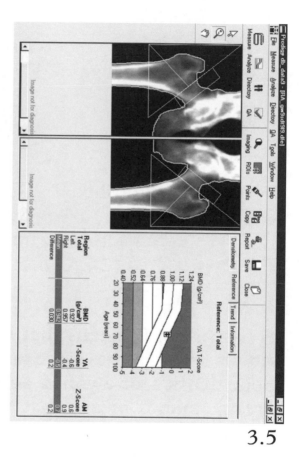

3.5

Ann's hipbone-density study. This is a DualFemur study, in which both hips are scanned. The bone density for the total region of the right and left hips is shown on the bottom right. The "mean" value refers to the average bone density in the total region for the right and left hips combined.

63

World Health Organization (WHO)
T-Scores

Normal	T-score of -1 or better
Osteopenia (Low Bone Density)	T-score between -1 and -2.5
Osteoporosis	T-score of -2.5 or poorer
Severe or Established Osteoporosis	T-score of -2.5 or poorer fragility fracture

A T-score of 0 means that the bone density is exactly the same as the average bone density for a young adult. A T-score greater than 0 means that the bone density is higher than the average bone density of the young adult. A T-score of 0 or above is considered great. A T-score down to -1 is still considered normal. When the T-score falls below -1 osteopenia and osteoporosis can occur.

The complete hipbone-density study is shown in Figure 3.5. This is a DualFemur study. Bone densities were measured in each hip individually and then the results were combined to give an average value. On the right are the graph and numbers. Doctors look at the mean of both hips using The World Health Organization's guidelines, or WHO T-Score. My T-score is −0.5, or normal.

My bone-density tests over the last several years appear on page 66. Since these earlier tests were taken on a different machine, the Bone Mineral Density values are lower because the machines are calibrated differently, but the result was the same: I had osteopenia in 1996 and my T-score improved with medication, diet, and exercise. Doctors use the T-score to determine the diagnosis. Doctors can use both the T-score and the z-score to predict fracture risk. The actual bone density in g/cm² is used to follow my progress.

When I had my first spine bone-density test in 1996, the "scores" of my Bone Mineral Density at L1–L4 fit the Women's Health Organization diagnosis of osteopenia. Also, my femoral neck was osteopenic. If I had taken no action, my bone densities would have continued to decline and my risk for fracture would have increased. Since I started my program of medicine, diet, and exercise, the tests show I have succeeded in stabilizing my bone density.

Figure 3.6 on page 67 is an image of my spine viewed from the side. The photo is used to evaluate the shapes of the verte-

Governor Richards's Spine Bone-Density Test from 1996–2001

Date	BMD (g/cm²)	T-Score
12/11/1996	0.915	-1.20
12/16/1997	0.920	-1.16
02/16/1999	0.855	-1.75
03/19/2001	0.908	-1.26

Governor Richards's Hipbone-Density Results from 1996–2001

Date	BMD (g/cm²)	Total Hip T-Score	BMD (g/cm²)	Femoral Neck T-Score
12/11/1996	0.859	-0.68	0.736	-1.02
12/16/1997	0.864	-0.64	0.751	-0.88
02/16/1999	0.840	-0.84	0.723	-1.14
03/19/2001	0.850	-0.75	0.756	-0.84

brae (whether they are "wedges" or not) to see if there are any fractures.

The front and back heights of the vertebrae can be compared and a diagnosis of fractures made.

Once a decision to have a bone-density test has been made, the doctor and patient need to consider which test to take — the spine and hip? The forearm? Bone density is measured with DEXA, which stands for Dual Energy X ray Absorptiometry. Most doctors agree that the gold standard is to do a DEXA scan of the spine and hip.

The national average reimbursement by Medicare for a spine or hip study in 2002 was $127.42. Medicaid programs also

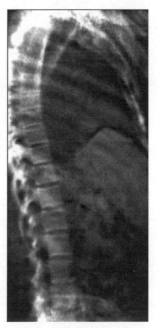

Ann's spine, viewed from the side. This is a lateral spine image that was obtained with the Prodigy bone densitometer. It can be used to diagnose spine fractures, just as a doctor would use a regular back X ray. Fortunately, Ann does not have any fractures in her spine.

3.6

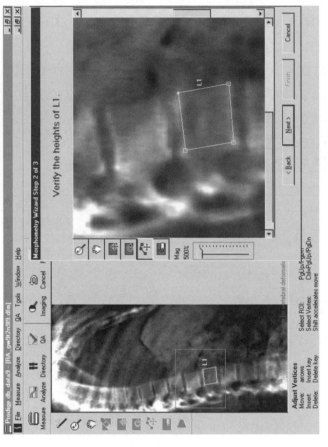

3.7

A close-up view of the upper portion of Ann's lower, or lumbar, spine. The dimensions of the vertebrae can be measured with computer technology.

cover bone-density measurements, although the reimbursement rates are more difficult to determine than for Medicare. In Indiana, reimbursement for a spine- or hipbone-density test under Medicaid was $52.60, while in Wisconsin it was $130.43. Managed-care organizations tend to reimburse at a higher rate, but exact rates are not available.

From the standpoint of the quality of my life for the rest of my life, the test was priceless. Every woman should talk to her doctor. Who raises the subject of bone density and osteoporosis does not matter, only that a conversation about protecting bones takes place. In addition, make sure your doctor measures your height at every physical. If you lose height, it might be a sign of osteoporosis and should be checked out further. No adult is too young to be educated about osteoporosis.

CHAPTER 4

WHAT IS OSTEOPOROSIS?

When I told my aunt Oleta that I was writing a book on osteoporosis, her immediate response was that everyone shrinks and it is just a part of getting old. Nursery-rhyme books invariably have illustrations of a little old lady with white hair, a cane, and a widow's hump. All of these characteristics are supposed to be signs of old age, but today that cane and widow's hump do not have to be a part of getting older.

Osteoporosis is a potentially fatal, progressive disease. We are not told that it is a disease with solutions. We are conditioned to think it is under that large umbrella called "Advanced Years," but this is incorrect. The humped back, shuffling walk, shrinking, and breaking bones is not part and parcel of aging; it is a disease. It was not until 1999 that a truly modern discussion of osteoporosis as a preventable and treatable disease appeared.

Gallup Survey

In May 2000, the National Osteoporosis Foundation announced the results of a Gallup survey of 1,039
women with osteoporosis. Even among
these women with osteoporosis, 46 percent still believed that osteoporosis was
an unavoidable part of aging for
women. Eighty-six percent said that
they had never talked to their doctor
about the prevention of osteoporosis
before they were diagnosed. Even after
being diagnosed, 48 percent of these
women were still not aware of the medications that arc available to reduce the
risk of fractures. Now that they already
have osteoporosis, 91 percent wished
they had taken the necessary steps to
prevent the disease.

The National Osteoporosis Foundation (NOF), the European Foundation for
Osteoporosis and Bone Disease, and the
National Institute for Arthritis and Mus-
culoskeletal and Skin Diseases have
agreed on this definition: "Osteoporosis
is a disease characterized by low bone

mass and microarchitectural deterioration of bone tissue leading to enhanced bone fragility and a consequent increase in fracture risk." This definition states that osteoporosis is a disease rather than a predictable and acceptable condition. And nowhere does it mention aging as a factor.

I have learned from Dr. Levine that osteoporosis is a change in the strength, or density, of the bones so that their consistency becomes porous, weblike, and more fragile. Osteoporosis literally means "porous bones."

Bone is living tissue. As living tissue, bone cells are constantly tearing down old or damaged bone in a process called "bone resorption" and then making new bone in a process called "bone formation." This breaking down and creating of new bone is called "bone remodeling." During childhood and particularly adolescence, there is more new bone being made than

---

Density, or strength of bones, is related to the concentration of minerals in the bones, mostly calcium. Most American women have been calcium deficient for more than a decade by the time they reach thirty.

---

there is old bone being removed. A woman's bone density will continue to increase as long as bone formation outpaces bone resorption. In general, 98 or 99 percent of the peak bone density will have been achieved by the time a woman is twenty. However, the National Institutes of Health (NIH) states that it is important to acknowledge a common misperception that osteoporosis is always the result of bone loss. Bone loss commonly occurs as men and women age; however, an individual who does not reach optimal (i.e., peak) bone mass during childhood and adolescence may develop osteoporosis without the occurrence of accelerated bone loss. This means that the failure to reach optimal or peak bone mass in childhood and adolescence is as responsible as bone loss for the development of osteoporosis. See page 157, Kids and Their Bones.

After peak bone density is reached, the process of bone formation and bone resorption are supposed to be balanced, or coupled. When bone formation and bone resorption are no longer balanced or uncoupled, and if bone loss goes on long enough, osteopenia and ultimately osteoporosis can occur. In the spine, in other-

In a report issued in 2002, the National Osteoporosis Foundation estimated that 44 million, or 55 percent, of men and woman age fifty and older in the United States have osteopenia or osteoporosis. This number is expected to reach 52 million by 2010, and 61 million by 2020.

wise healthy women, bone density remains fairly constant between the ages of twenty and forty-five. In the hip, uncoupling may occur even sooner, causing very minimal bone loss that begins as early as a woman's thirties.

There are factors that make us more vulnerable to osteoporosis, such as some medications contributing to bone loss. For example, I began to have seizures after Ellen, my fourth child, was born. The doctor put me on Dilantin, which contributes to bone loss, but at the time the seizures were more serious than the threat of bone loss. After many years, I was able to go off the medicine without having seizures. The Dilantin may have contributed to my bone loss, but there are other factors, too, like smoking, alcohol consumption, and calcium deficiency.

Following are factors that may increase vulnerability to osteoporosis or fractures:

LOW BODY WEIGHT — LESS THAN 127 POUNDS
LOW BONE MINERAL DENSITY (BMD)
MENSTRUAL HISTORY
  Amenorrhea — early and sporadic loss of periods
  Premature menopause
  Postmenopausal estrogen deficiency

LIFESTYLE
  Sedentary
  Excessive exercising while young (gymnasts, dancers, runners)
  Cigarette smoking
  Alcoholism

PERSONAL AND FAMILY HISTORY
  Female
  Family history of osteoporosis
  Family history of hip fracture
  Advanced age
  Caucasian, Hispanic, or Asian
  History of fragility fracture after age 45

(continued)

DIET
  Inadequate calcium/vitamin D

DISEASES
  Eating disorders — anorexia and
    bulimia
  Intestinal disorders — malabsorp-
    tion, celiac disease, Crohn's disease
  Gastrectomy
  Hyperthyroidism
  Hyperparathyroidism
  Multiple sclerosis
  Thalassemia
  Severe liver disease
  Multiple myeloma

INCREASED RISK MAY BE DUE TO
TREATMENT OF THESE CONDITIONS
  Chronic inflammatory disease
    — rheumatoid arthritis
  Insulin-dependent diabetes
  Leukemia and lymphoma
  Endometriosis

DRUGS THAT CAN INCREASE
YOUR RISK
  Glucocorticoids (steroids)
  Aluminum-containing drugs

(continued)

Anticonvulsants
Cytotoxic drugs
GNRH-agonists-lupron, etc.
Heparin
Lithium
Excessive thyroid hormone
  replacement

INCREASED RISK OF FALLING AND
FRACTURE
  Cataracts
  Prone to falls
  Dementia
  Frailty
  Impaired balance
  Poor vision
  Sedatives

ADDITIONAL RISK FACTORS FOR HIP
FRACTURE
  Height greater than 5'7"
  Long hip axis length
  Any of the factors that increase risk

Osteoporosis causes 1.5 million fractures every year in the United States alone. Spine fractures are the most common, numbering around 700,000. There are 300,000 hip fractures each year, and

The most common locations of osteoporatic fractures are indicated by the arrows: the spine, the wrist, and the hip. IMAGE ADAPTED FROM ECLECTI-COLLECTIONS™

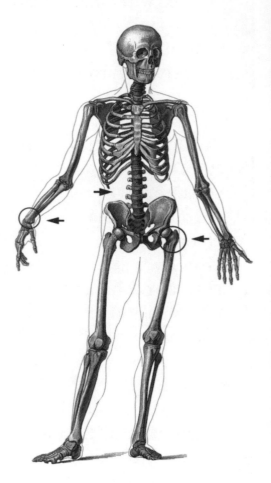

4.1

250,000 wrist fractures. Breaks in other bones caused by osteoporosis also number around 250,000. This includes fractures of the ribs, pelvis, arms, and ankles. The only fractures in older women that are not caused by osteoporosis are that are not caused by osteoporosis are broken toes and fingers

Because osteoporosis causes bones to become porous and brittle, fractures can occur. Dr. Levine says that fractures in the spine due to osteoporosis are the most common. Spine fractures can be found in women as early as their fifties. This is what causes the stooped posture and widow's hump. As the bones become porous, the spine begins to curve forward (this is called "kyphosis"). The vertebrae, the

4.2

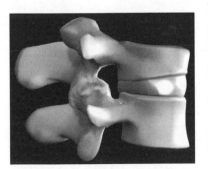

A compression fracture in the spine. The upper bone is wedge-shaped in comparison to the lower, normal-shaped bone.
ADAPTED FROM LIFEART IMAGE, © 2002, LIPPENCOTT WILLIAMS & WILKINS. ALL RIGHTS RESERVED.

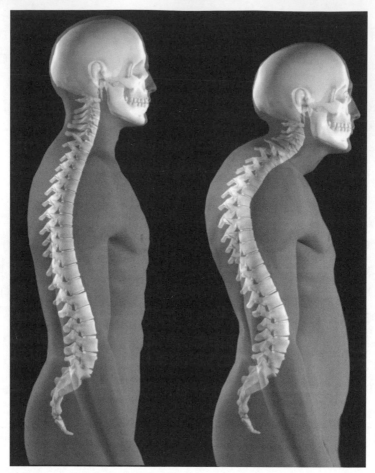

4.3

Normal spine curvature and kyphosis. The normal spine, on the left, becomes kyphotic, or bent forward, as multiple compression fractures in the spine develop. The pronounced forward curve in the upper back is often called a widow's hump or dowager's hump.

bones that make up the spine, do not actually break, they collapse. The bone is compressed from its usual square shape into a wedge, like a doorstop. And, since these bones can compress over a period of time rather than collapsing suddenly, the pain may be mild and mistaken for an everyday backache. Breaks in the wedge-shaped vertebrae can also occur abruptly, causing severe pain. The most severe pain results after a total collapse of the vertebra. Both the front and back of the bone are compressed, rather than just the front. This is called a crush fracture. Each of these compressions causes a loss in height.

Loss of height and the resulting posture causes the spine to bend forward. The heart, lungs, and intestinal tract then are

4.4

A wrist fracture may result when the arm is extended to break a fall.

pushed into a smaller space.

In May 2002, I was invited by Queen Rania of Jordan to speak at the Women's Leadership Roundtable at the International Osteoporosis Foundation meeting in Lisbon, Portugal. Camilla Parker Bowles, several other prominent women, Queen Rania, and I were all there to speak about osteoporosis. I had never heard the ravages of osteoporosis described as poignantly or eloquently as when Camilla Parker Bowles spoke about her mother's and her grand-mother's deaths. There was a point in her mother's life when she became so stooped that her intestines were compressed. She was in pain and it was very difficult for her to eat. Women think they cannot die from being stooped over, but they do.

Like me, people also break their arms and their wrists as a consequence of falls. They break their ankles and legs, too. And the sad thing about broken bones is that the healing period keeps people from doing the things they need to do; it can re-quire time off the job, or time away from family.

There is another cost to people with the disease. Osteoporosis can cause fear. Watch someone who has previously broken bones step off of a curb, exit a car, or rise from a chair. People afraid of breaking bones are tentative and cautious. They often shuffle instead of striding. Their gait communicates their confidence, or lack of it. I do not want to spend my time on this earth worrying whether I can make it off of the curb or not. When a person has to concentrate on movement, it is a mental drain.

Several years ago, I was admiring a group of parked motorcycles. I made a casual remark to someone that I wanted to ride a motorcycle on my sixtieth birthday. It turned out that there was a newspaper reporter standing nearby. The next thing I knew, newspapers all over the country picked up the story. Harley-Davidson sent me a big, beautiful, white Harley with a Texas flag on it! It was stunning. I took lessons to learn how to ride the new bike and I got my motorcycle license. Now the bike belongs to the state of Texas, but I like to think that if I got that motorcycle tomorrow, I would still not be afraid to ride it. Having the confidence that I can do anything I choose to do is an important part of mental health.

CHAPTER 5

MENOPAUSE, ESTROGEN, AND BONES

Women's bodies are designed to go through a period in which they mature and begin menstrual periods so that they can bear children. Later, there is a period in their lives when they can no longer bear children, and after which they are supposed to die. Medicine and science have outwitted this system.

Now, instead of menopause marking the beginning of the end of life, it really is the beginning of a brand-new life. It is a period of freedom and opportunity. When I think of my mother and her generation, I realize they did not have the second chance that we do now. They did not have the opportunity to enjoy a healthy, active, second or third act.

When I was growing up, menopause was treated like a joke. It was "all in your head," like craving pickles in pregnancy. Women did not talk about menopause

Life Expectancy

The life expectancy of a woman age fifty today is eighty-five years. This means women can expect to live a full third of their lives as postmenopausal women.

much because it would have been considered vulgar or crass. Sadly, there was also the suggestion that once a woman passed menopause, she was no longer physically desirable. Or worse yet, that the purpose of a woman's life had come and gone.

Although images of women with "perfect" figures are everywhere, I give magazines a lot of credit for bringing discussions about sex and sexuality out of the closet. Talking about sex, talking about desire, putting women on a par with men where sex is concerned, allowed us to talk about other subjects that were taboo, including menopause. Women have to feel secure enough to say, "I suffer from premenstrual syndrome. Sometimes the hormones in my body make the day more difficult for me." Or, "I am in the middle of menopause, and as a consequence, this room is a lot hotter for me than it is for you."

I do not know how old I was when I went through menopause, but I do not think I had a menstrual period after I was forty-eight. Like a lot of women, I just noticed that my periods were fewer and fewer. I had a very easy menopause compared to a lot of women. I have friends

Why Does a Woman's Period Stop?

Periods stop because of a process called "follicular atresia" in the ovaries. In plain English, that means that the follicles that contain the eggs within the ovaries die. No one knows why the follicles die, but they do. When there are no more healthy follicles to produce eggs, menstrual periods stop. The number of follicles a woman has begins to fall even before her menstrual period starts and continues falling throughout her adulthood. After the age of forty, the follicles die at a faster rate and, by the time menopause occurs, only a few thousand remain.

Hot Flashes

Hot flashes were not seriously studied by the medical profession until 1975. When they finally were, it became clear that hot flashes and night sweats were the result of the body's temperature regulatory mechanisms running amok in the absense of enough estrogen. When scientists measure body temperature in the inner ear and rectum during a hot flash, they find that the temperature actually goes up several degrees. This causes about a ten-degree rise in the skin temperature. The sensation can last for five to ten minutes In the United States, about 76 percent of postmeno- pausal women experience hot flashes, most for more than a year and many for more than five years after menopause.

who have really been through an absolute hell, but I was fortunate and only had a few hot flashes.

Part of the reason my menopause was so mild may have been because I started on hormone replacement even before it had begun. I took Premarin and Provera for a long time, maybe twenty years. I was still on estrogen replacement therapy when I started on medication for osteoporosis. Back then, I had no hesitation about taking estrogen. Today, however, I would talk over the benefits and risks associated with estrogen with my doctor.

The knowledge that menopause and osteoporosis were related has been around since 1941. Drs. Fuller Albright, Patricia Smith, and Anna Richardson wrote in the *Journal of the American Medical Association* that the "postmenopausal state" was the most common cause of osteoporosis.

At menopause, the bone loss in the spine is rapid and may continue for up to ten years before it begins to slow. Bone loss may actually accelerate again in women in their seventies — not only from the spine but from the hip as well. In one study, a loss of 10.5 percent from the spine was

Medically speaking, menopause is the last menstrual period. Of course, most women do not realize that a particular period was the last one. The average age of the last menstrual period is fifty-one years, and this age has not changed much through all of recorded history.

Why the Lack of Estrogen Can Cause Bone Loss

How the lack of estrogen causes bone loss is a matter of intense research. Estrogen attaches to some of the cells within the bone at sites called "estrogen receptors." When the ovary stops producing estrogen and these estrogen receptor sites are left vacant, the bone cells produce excessive amounts of substances called "cytokines." Some of these cytokines cause bone loss. When estrogen is replaced and the estrogen receptor sites on the bone are again filled, the production of the cytokines decreases, stopping bone loss. Not surprisingly, if estrogen replacement is stopped, bone loss begins again. The relationship between estrogen, cytokines, and bone loss is extremely complex. In essence, estrogen acts as a regulator of the production of cytokines by the bones. The estrogen deficiency that occurs at menopause leaves the production of these substances unregulated. The result is bone loss.

seen within four years of menopause. In another study, 20–25 percent of bone density was lost from the spine and hip within sixteen years of menopause. Depending on whether a doctor looks at the spine, hip, or wrist, women lose 15–45 percent of their bone density over a lifetime.

Every woman should discuss menopause, not just osteoporosis, with her doctor. And surprisingly that conversation should begin in your early forties, the pre- and perimenopausal years. By starting that young, you will not only become better informed, but you will be able to make lifestyle changes that will improve your health and prevent certain diseases. In these conversations with your doctor the role of hormone replacement therapy (HRT) and how it will impact your personal health profile should be a cornerstone decision. The issue is not just how HRT reduces the risk for osteoporosis (it does), but whether it also reduces your risk of other debilitating diseases.

The decision about whether to begin a course of HRT treatment got a lot more complicated in 2002. That was the year the results of the Women's Health Initiative (WHI) were released ahead of schedule to the national media. WHI, a huge national study looking at the effects of Prempro, a combined estrogen (Premarin) and progestin (Provera) HRT, cited some negative findings linking use of this drug to risk for breast cancer and heart disease (See box, below.)

The Women's Health Initiative

The Women's Health Initiative (WHI) is an ongoing study sponsored by the National Institutes of Health launched in 1991 to investigate among other issues any possible association between the use of HRT's and the increased risk of diseases in otherwise healthy, postmenopausal women. In 2002 one portion of this study was suddenly suspended after five years, when a group of women randomized to take Prempro, a combination of Premarin and Provera, showed a 26 percent increase in invasive breast cancer and a 22 percent increase in risk for coronary heart disease. The WHI study is the first rigorously designed and randomized (continued) controlled trial to explore these casual links. The announcement of the findings and immediate halt to this arm of the investgation made news in all media outlets from television to print. While these percentages are significant, the actual numbers need to be considered. There were eight additional cases of breast cancer per 10,000 women per year compared to those women on placebos (38 versus 30) and seven more cases of coronary heart disease per 10,000 women per year (37 versus 30).

Despite these negative indicators, there was good news with respect to osteoporosis. Risk for vertebral and hip fractures was reduced. Hip fractures were lowered by 34 percent or five per 10,000 women per year (10 versus 15). This is the largest clinical trial to date to show the protective effect of HRT on hip fractures. The study also reported a 37 percent decrease in colorectal cancer for the women taking HRT or six fewer cases per 10,000 (10 versus 16).

When I began hormone replacement twenty years ago, there were far fewer choices to consider than there are today. I took Premarin and Provera because that is what was recommended to me at the time. I took them to help with any unpleasant side effects of menopause. Today, there are many other brands and forms of hormone replacement. Since I was taking Premarin and Provera before menopause and still have osteopenia, I cannot say with any certainty how the drugs affected my bone loss. Similarly, the hormone replacement regimen that was considered "standard" twenty years ago is used far less often today. There are a lot of choices and much more to consider now than when my doctor recommended I begin hormone replacement therapy. Every woman should talk with her own doctor.

A FEW IMPORTANT DEFINITIONS:

Estrogen: Refers to all of the various forms of estrogen such as estradiol, estrone, ethinyl estradiol, and conjugated equine estrogen. Estrogen can mean any or all of these different chemical forms of estrogen no matter how they are taken.

Progestin: Refers to any synthetic form of progesterone.

Progestogen: Refers to both the synthetic progestins and natural progesterone.

HRT: If a woman takes both estrogen and a progestin/progestogen after menopause, she is said to be taking hormone replacement therapy, or HRT.

ERT: If a woman takes estrogen only, then she is said to be taking estrogen replacement therapy, or ERT.

Remember, HRT and ERT explain whether a woman is taking estrogen alone or estrogen and a progestogen, but the terms do not specify the type or brand of hormone she is taking or how.

Dr. Levine says there are three major forms of estrogen made in the human body. After menopause, estrogens used for hormone replacement are natural or synthetic. Natural means that the particular form of estrogen is found in nature. It does not necessarily mean that the particular estrogen is normally found in the human body. Synthetic, of course, means that the estrogen was created in a laboratory. Many forms of postmenopausal estrogen replacement began as plant estrogens. One of the oldest and best-known forms of postmenopausal estrogen replacement, Premarin, which is what I took, comes from horses. These are considered natural estrogens because they are found in nature, obviously not because they are specifically found in the human body. Ethinyl estradiol, on the other hand, is a very potent synthetic estrogen. This is the type of estrogen found in most birth-control pills, but it is also used in small amounts for postmenopausal hormone replacement.

Estrogens can be further divided into categories based on how they are administered. There are oral, parenteral, or vaginal estrogens. *Oral estrogens* are any type of estrogen in a pill taken by mouth. *Parenteral estrogens* are estrogens that are given in an injection or absorbed directly through the skin. Estrogen injections are seldom used today as part of a postmenopausal hormone replacement. In the United States, the most common method for delivering estrogen through the skin is with a patch. Estrogen creams and gels applied to the skin are other forms of parenteral estrogens. The phrase "transdermal estrogen" generally refers to an estrogen patch, although it could be used to describe estrogen creams or gels applied to the skin. *Vaginal estrogens* are estrogens that are placed directly in the vagina. Estrogen creams have been the predominant form of vaginal estrogen, but in recent years, very small vaginal estrogen tablets have become available as well as an estrogen ring. Vaginal estrogens are most often used to treat vaginal dryness from estrogen deficiency rather than general hormone replacement. They may be used alone or in combination with oral or parenteral estrogen replacement.

Like estrogens, progestogens can be classified as natural or synthetic, but progesterone is really the only natural progestogen. Everything else is synthetic. Progestogens can also be divided into oral or parenteral forms, but few parenteral progestogens are available.

Progestins are divided into two chemical categories depending on their similarity to progesterone itself or testosterone, the major male sex hormone. These are sometimes called C-17 progestins and 19-nor progestins, respectively. Provera, which is what I used, is a C-17 progestin called medroxyprogesterone acetate.

Progestogens can cause side effects such

as breast tenderness, bloating, leg swelling, and abdominal cramping. About 5 percent of women simply cannot tolerate progestogens no matter which one they use. In the remaining 95 percent, it is a matter of finding the right one. If a woman is using a C-17 progestin and having difficulties, a 19-nor progestin can be tried, and vice versa.

When estrogen is given by itself, this is called unopposed estrogen. Without progesterone, which women normally have as premenopausal women, the stimulation of the uterus lining (endometrium) by estrogen can go unchecked and lead to the development of endometrial cancer. What doctors know now is that when a progestogen is added for part of the menstrual cycle, as it normally is during the cycle of a premenopausal woman, there is no increase in the risk of endometrial cancer for a postmenopausal woman taking estrogen replacement. If a woman has had a hysterectomy, which is the surgical removal of the uterus, then progestogen is not prescribed. A postmenopausal woman with an intact uterus who takes estrogen should always take a progestogen. If there is some overwhelming reason that a woman cannot take a progestogen, but is taking estrogen anyway, she must undergo regular and frequent testing to detect the early signs of endometrial cancer.

Dr. Levine Explains What Schedule or Regimen a Woman Should Use, If She Decides to Take ERT or HRT:

In talking about hormone replacement regimens, the particular type of estrogen or progestogen does not matter — only how many days a month a woman uses either or both of them.

CYCLICAL HORMONE REPLACEMENT:

In cyclical hormone replacement, estrogen is given every day. Progestogen is added for a total of ten to fourteen days each month and some menstrual bleeding will occur after the progestogen is stopped. A woman decides when to add the progestogen, and if she begins the progestogen on the first of the month, she can expect bleeding around the middle of the month or she can begin the progestogen around the fifteenth, in which case the bleeding will occur at the end of the month or the first of the next. Of women following cyclical hormone replacement, 85 percent experience bleeding. Even though hormones used in this manner cause menstrual periods to continue, a woman cannot become pregnant. Becoming pregnant requires that a follicle in the ovary releases an egg. Postmenopausal hormone replacement does not cause this to happen.

COMBINED-CONTINUOUS HORMONE REPLACEMENT:

The nuisance of ongoing menstrual periods is a major reason that many women stop hormone replacement. In the combined-continuous hormone replacement regimen, estrogen is again taken every day. The progestogen is also taken every day instead of just ten to fourteen days a month, as in the cyclical regimens. The dose of the progestogen is generally smaller than that used in the cyclical regimen. The intended result is no bleeding. Unfortunately, the combined-continuous regimen is not 100 percent successful in this regard. In the first six months that a woman uses combined-continuous hormone replacement, some bleeding is expected, and it can be sporadic and unpredictable. After the first six months, though, more and more women have no more bleeding. The percentage of women who do not bleed by the end of one year of therapy is still not 100 percent, but it has been reported to be as high as 80 percent, depending on the particular product or products used.

PILLS OR PATCHES?

Once a woman and her doctor have decided on a particular regimen, the question becomes which estrogen and, for women with that "intact uterus," which progestogen should she use? For the last fifty years, oral estrogens have been the mainstay of estrogen replacement. Transdermal estrogen patches are gaining in popularity and acceptance. Both the pills and the patches work extremely well to relieve the symptoms of estrogen deficiency and prevent potential long-term consequences. There are potentially different health concerns between pills and patches that may influence a woman's choice, so every woman should consult her doctor on the risks and benefits of each.

Deciding to use ERT or HRT is a matter of weighing the potential benefits and risks as well as choosing the preparations and regimen that suits each woman best. It is important to look at the entire picture. A

Estrogen-Containing Preparations That Are FDA Approved for the Prevention of Osteoporosis.

Brand Name	Minimum Dose for Prevention of Osteoporosis	Oral or Patch
Premarin	0.625mg	Oral
Ogen	0.625mg	Oral
Estrace	0.5mg	Oral
Estratab	0.3mg	Oral
Ortho-Est	0.625mg	Oral
Estraderm	0.05mg	Patch
Climara	0.025mg	Patch
Vivelle	0.025mg	Patch

Estrogen/Androgen Preparations That Are FDA Approved for the Prevention of Osteoporosis. There Is Only 1 Dose Available for Each Preparation.

Brand Name	Oral or Patch
Estratest	Oral
Estratest HS	Oral

Estrogen/Progestin Preparations That Are FDA Approved for the Prevention of Osteoporosis.
There are two formulations of Prempro that differ in the amount of progestin. There is only one dose formulation available for each of the remaining products.

Brand Name	Oral or Patch
Premphase	Oral
Prempro	Oral
Ortho-Prefest	Oral
Femhrt	Oral
Activella	Oral

woman's choice among preparations has increased dramatically in the last few years. Finding the right preparation and regimen, however, may be a bit of trial and error.

Not all of the pills and patches available have been approved by the FDA for the prevention of osteoporosis. Even if a woman is taking an FDA-approved hormone, it is important to know if the dose she is taking is one that has been shown to stop bone loss. FDA-approved preparations are shown on pages 101–02.

The list of preparations that are FDA approved is growing rapidly as more studies are done. The lists here may not include drugs approved by the FDA since the writing of this book.

Some preparations are not approved for the *treatment* of bone loss, but they are approved for the *prevention* of osteoporosis. What that means is the preparation reduces the risk of fracture. As an example, Premarin was FDA approved for the treatment of osteoporosis, but was taken off the list as it did not measure up to modern studies. It is, however, FDA approved for prevention.

If a woman decides not to use ERT or HRT, she should not forget about her bones. If she does nothing, she will lose bone mass. There are nonestrogen medications that are FDA approved for the prevention of osteoporosis that a woman can use to protect her bones. These medications are explored in Chapter 7. A decision not to use estrogen replacement does not have to be a roll of the dice when it comes to developing osteoporosis.

Last summer I was walking down Madison Avenue when I tripped over a piece of plywood and literally fell on my face.

I found myself looking up at a man I had never seen before who was trying to help me. "I am fine," I said, "I will just dust myself off."

"No, lady, you are hurt pretty badly," he said. I touched my head and sure enough there was blood, lots of it.

"Who are you?" I asked.

He was an EMT worker and I realized there was an ambulance at the curb. "Well, gosh, how lucky I am that you were here on this corner."

"Yes, we brought the ambulance to pick up another woman who fell at this same spot and broke her elbow."

I got in the ambulance with the woman who had fallen before me and had broken her arm. And bless her heart, I stole all the thunder because she was not bleeding and she had never been a governor. I needed twenty stitches and plastic surgery to improve the mobility of my eyebrow, but thank goodness I did not break one bone. I feel certain that I would have broken a bone if I had not made the serious effort to address my osteopenia.

My mother had recently broken her arm in this photo with my son, Clark, his wife, Sharon, and baby Maeve in 1996.
ANN RICHARD'S PERSONAL COLLECTION

Here I am, future governor of the State of Texas, at age six.
ANN RICHARD'S PERSONAL COLLECTION

With my mother on high school graduation day on the front porch of the house she built in Waco. ANN W. RICHARD'S PAPERS, CENTER FOR AMERICAN HISTORY, UNIVERSITY OF TEXAS, AUSTIN, TX

On my wedding day, with my parents. ANN W. RICHARD'S PAPERS, CENTER FOR AMERICAN HISTORY, UNIVERSITY OF TEXAS, AUSTIN, TX

My parents, Iona and Cecil Wills. ANN W. RICHARD'S PAPERS, CENTER FOR AMERICAN HISTORY, UNIVERSITY OF TEXAS, AUSTIN, TX

My maternal grandparents, Eula and Hosea Warren. ANN RICHARD'S PERSONAL COLLECTION

My paternal grandmother Alta Wills, whom I called Nanny. ANN RICHARD'S PERSONAL COLLECTION

My parents, Iona and Cecil Wills, during my second campaign for Governor in 1994. My father gradually lost his eyesight during the '90s. ANN W. RICHARD'S PAPERS, CENTER FOR AMERICAN HISTORY, UNIVERSITY OF TEXAS, AUSTIN, TX

My grandchildren. Behind me, from left to right, are Daniel, Hannah, and Jennifer. Next to me is Lily.

My oldest daughter Cecile and me and my first grandchild, Lily.

Standing, left to right: daughter Ellen Richards, son-in-law Greg Johnson, son-in-law Kirk Adams, daughter Cecile Richards, daughter-in-law Linda Richards, son Dan Richards, daughter- in-law Sharon Richards, and son Clark Richards. Sitting, left to right: granddaughter Hannah Adams, grandson Wyatt Richards, granddaughter Lily Adams, Ann Richards, granddaughter Samantha Richards, granddaughter Jen- nifer Richards, granddaughter Maeve Richards, and grandson Daniel Adams.

CHAPTER 6

BONE BREAKERS: CAFFEINE, TOBACCO, ALCOHOL

As a young married woman I drank coffee and alcohol and smoked cigarettes, and if someone had told me that they might damage my bones, I am not sure I would have stopped. We did not think much about protecting our bones then since stooped postures and unexplained fractures were the province of aging. I smoked until the 80s and drank to excess until my family and friends intervened. I went to "drunk school" at St. Mary's Hospital in Minneapolis where they treated me for alcoholism. Because of Alcoholics Anonymous and the support of my family and friends, this year I will celebrate twenty-three years of sobriety. I started drinking coffee in my early twenties. I still drink about four cups a day, but now it is decaffeinated. When I got off caffeine, I had a headache for three days.

Caffeine

Though caffeine is a natural substance, it is also considered a chemical compound. It belongs to the chemical family known as methylxanthines. Caffeine is a stimulant for the heart and brain, which is the good news. Unfortunately, caffeine also affects how our bodies handle calcium.

Calcium is the most important and abundant mineral found in our bones. People have to consume calcium because our bodies cannot manufacture it, but no matter how much calcium an individual consumes, a certain percentage will be lost from the body in the urine. Early research suggested that caffeine could increase these losses. Since people tend to consume less calcium than they need, anything that increased their daily loss was a cause for concern.

In 1995, Drs. Barger-Lux and Heaney reviewed 560 studies of calcium and caffeine in women 34 to 69. They concluded that for every 6oz of caffeinated coffee consumed, the body's calcium stores went down 4.6mg a day, but to offset this, all that was needed was to increase the dietary intake of calcium by 40mg a day. Two tablespoons of milk in a cup of coffee will do that.

Tables 1–3 provide information to help moderate caffeine intake. Serving sizes are important: a regular coffee cup usually holds 5–6oz of liquid; a mug holds 12oz; a standard size can of soda is a 12oz serving. The United States Food and Drug Administration (FDA) limits the amount of caffeine in carbonated beverages to a maximum of 6mg per ounce so the maximum a 12oz can will have is 72mg. Some over-the-counter pain medications also contain caffeine in significant amounts — be sure to read the medication label. Note that cocoa, chocolate candies, and Coffee Nips have very little caffeine. Try to limit the intake of caffeine to 300mg a day or less. Use this basic rule of thumb: limit caffeine intake to three servings of a caffeinated food and beverage each day. After three servings of caffeine, switch to decaf. Combine this with adequate calcium, and caffeine will not be a problem.

Table 1: Caffeine Content of a 5oz Mug or Serving of Common Hot Beverages

Coffee

Drip	110–150mg
Percolated	64–124mg
Instant	40–108mg
Decaffeinated	2–5mg
Instant Decaffeinated	2mg

Hot Tea

1-minute brew	9–33mg
3-minute brew	20–46mg
5-minute brew	20–50mg
Instant	12–28mg

Cocoa	4mg

U.S. Food and Drug Administration and National Soft Drink Association

Remember — try to limit the intake of caffeine to 300mg a day.

Table 2: Caffeine Content of 12oz Servings of Various Soft Drinks and Cold Teas

Soft Drinks

Coca-Cola Classic	34mg
Diet Coke	45mg
Dr Pepper	41mg
Diet Dr Pepper	41mg
A & W Cream Soda	29mg
Sunkist Orange Soda	41mg
Mountain Dew	55mg
Diet Mountain Dew	55mg
Pepsi-Cola	38mg
Diet Pepsi-Cola	36mg
Pepsi One	55mg
Royal Crown Soda	43mg
Barq's Root Beer	22mg
A & W Root Beer	0mg
Mug Root Beer	0mg
Sprite	0mg
7-Up	0mg

Teas

Snapple Teas (all flavors)	8–32mg
Lipton Brisk Teas (all flavors)	9mg
Nestea (different varieties)	6–26mg

U.S. Food and Drug Administration and National Soft Drink Association

Table 3: Caffeine Content of Frozen Coffee Desserts and Various Candies

Frozen Coffee Desserts

Ben & Jerry's No Fat Coffee Fudge Frozen Yogurt	1 cup	85mg
Starbucks Coffee Ice Cream, various flavors	1 cup	40-60mg
Haagen-Dazs Coffee Ice Cream	1 cup	58mg
Haagen-Dazs Coffee Frozen Yogurt, fat free	1 cup	40mg
Starbuck's Frappuccino Bar	1 bar (2.5oz)	15mg

Chocolates/Candies

Hershey's Special Dark Chocolate Bar	1 bar (1.5oz)	31mg
Hershey's Milk Chocolate Bar	1 bar (1.5oz)	10mg
Coffee Nips	2 pieces	6mg

Center for Science in the Public Interest

I would smoke tomorrow if I could. I have kicked other habits, but smoking is the most insidious. I smoked like a stove, and when I was young, we used to sneak cigarettes. We thought smoking was cool. Mama did not smoke; she hated it. And she would make me blow my breath into her face when I came home from a date to see if I had been smoking. I quit many times, but I finally stopped in the late 1980s. I quit because it is a downright nasty habit and makes everything — your clothes, your home — smell bad. It is just an unpleasant substance. I also quit because I was afraid I would get lung cancer.

Smoking adds ten years to the age of your bones. When you stop, although the damage stops, it could take ten years to undo it. Smoking increases your risk for osteoporosis several ways. It effects the ovaries and the estrogen they produce, and it affects a woman's ability to absorb calcium.

In a healthy premenopausal woman, the ovary is the most important source of estrogen in the body. The major type of estrogen made by the ovary is called estradiol. Another form is estrone. Estrone

Can Smoking Accelerate Menopause?

In 1985, a study of over 7,800 women clearly showed that women who smoked became menopausal 1.74 years earlier than women who did not smoke. A second medical study published a year later suggested that women who smoked became menopausal even sooner, some 2.2 years earlier than women who do not smoke. *Women who did not smoke but husbands did also became menopausal at an earlier age.* Why smoking causes an earlier menopause is not known with certainty, but it is theorized that smoking accelerates the death of the egg-producing follicles in the ovaries. When enough follicles have died, the ovary quits producing estrogen and the menstral periods stop. What this means of course is that women who smoke or whose husbands smoke become estrogen deficient some two years earlier than they would otherwise.

can be converted to estradiol and vice versa in the liver. Estradiol is, by far, the more potent estrogen. Estradiol and estrone circulate in the blood in order to reach the various tissues in the body, including bone. Women who smoke make less estrogen than women who do not. Researchers have found, by studying identical twins, that women who smoke one pack of cigarettes a day throughout their adult lives will have a 5–10 percent lower bone density by the time they reach menopause.

In a three-year study of 402 older men and women in the United States, calcium absorption was significantly lower in

Smoking Affects ERT

The effects of smoking on estrogen are not limited to estrogen made in the body. If a postmenopausal woman takes oral estrogen replacement and smokes, the smoking will reduce the effectiveness to the estrogen replacement in protecting her bones. Studies have found that smokers have no protection from hip fracture by ERT while nonsmokers do have this protection.

smokers than in nonsmokers. Even when calcium and vitamin D supplements were given, the smokers still absorbed less calcium than the nonsmokers. In this study, the smokers also lost bone at the hip at a faster rate than nonsmokers. A more rapid bone loss from the wrist has also been demonstrated in smokers, and these effects occur in people who smoke less than one pack a day.

Studies that have compared the bone density and risk for fractures between smokers and nonsmokers have found that

Free Radicals

Smoking is known to increase the concentration of cancer-causing elements in the body called "free radicals." Free radicals have been implicated in a variety of diseases and the aging process in general. They may also cause bone loss through a direct effect on the bone. Some researchers have advocated antioxidant vitamins to offset this effect, but it would obviously be better to stop smoking.

smokers have lower bone densities and higher risk for fractures, particularly hip fractures. One of the largest long-range studies of a controlled group is the Nurses' Health Study. The effects of smoking and hip fracture risk have been published based on following 116,229 female nurses for twelve years. Women who smoked had a 30 percent greater risk of hip fracture than nonsmokers. The more a woman smoked, the greater was her risk. If a woman smoked twenty-five cigarettes or more a day, her risk was 60 percent greater.

Alcohol

I have written of my alcoholism in *Straight from the Heart*. I was treated for alcoholism in 1980 at St. Mary's Hospital in Minneapolis, and have not had the urge to drink alcohol since. By the grace of God and Alcoholics Anonymous, I celebrated twenty-two years of sobriety last year. Some good things other than sobriety came out of this period of my life. The positive effects it had on my family are enough for an entire book. Also, it caused me to take some positive actions when I was governor, such as passing legislation that established substance-abuse treatment in state prisons. The connection between alcoholism and crime needs no further elaboration. It is common knowledge that more than 80 percent of all crime is committed by individuals under the influence of alcohol or illegal drugs. The program was designed to equip inmates for life following their release from prison, and we worked with inmates and their families because the support of family is essential to recovery. It was an innovative and successful attempt to deal with addiction and recidivism. I even attended AA meetings with inmates in one of the prisons.

Before I worked with Dr. Levine, I knew only that alcohol abuse was related to osteoporosis, though I did not know how. Alcohol abuse is hazardous for bones because it inhibits the construction of new bone cells and as a result our bone density thins.

The levels of bone-forming cells are lower in individuals who consume too much alcohol, giving further strength to the belief that alcohol impairs bone formation. Individuals who develop cirrhosis of the liver from alcohol abuse have lower levels of vitamin D and lower levels of sex hormones. A lack of vitamin D will affect the ability to absorb calcium from the diet and the result can be bone loss. Lower levels of sex hormones, like estrogen in women and testosterone in men, can also cause bone loss as explained in Chapter 5.

When bone density in the spine and hip has been measured in chronic alcoholics, it has almost always been found to be lower than in healthy individuals of the same age and sex. Research has shown that with abstinence, the bones' ability to make new bone cells can recover.

Moderation means no more than one alcoholic beverage a day. Ideally, any alcohol consumption should be followed by two or three days of abstinence so the various organ systems that are affected by alcohol have a chance to recover.

CHAPTER 7

BONE HELPERS: CALCIUM, VITAMINS, PRESCRIPTION MEDICATIONS FOR PREVENTION AND TREATMENT

I was encouraged to take vitamin supplements when I was growing up since my father worked for a wholesale drug company. When I was a child, we always had a cow, but no refrigeration, just an icebox — which was literally a box with a place for a block of ice on top. The fresh milk I drank was always warm and I hated it. My mother would say, "Drink your milk and stop whining." I do not think she would have considered serving chocolate milk, even if we could afford it. Mama thought that drinking milk was a duty, not a pleasure. And so did I, but I am sure I never drank milk once I reached high school age. Since I do not like milk, I have to find creative ways to drink it. I drink nonfat milk with my cereal every morning. I drink coffee with nonfat milk all day long. I add yogurt to smoothies and eat nonfat yogurt for dessert. In short, I trick myself into eating calcium-rich dairy products.

Calcium

The vitamins and minerals, including calcium, that we need to strengthen our bones and later in life to keep their density are inexpensive and accessible. As a matter of fact, an 8oz glass of whole milk a day contains about one-third of the necessary calcium. Skim milk contains even more. But when was the last time anyone drank

In the 1990s, a study was done of 1,100 adolescents to determine what they knew about calcium and how much they were consuming. Of these kids, 90 percent believed that calcium was important to strengthen bones and 60 percent said they knew that adolescence was a critical period for strengthening their bones. The majority said that dairy products were the main source of dietary calcium. But the bad news was that researchers found that most teenage girls were consuming only 45 percent of the recommended daily amount of calcium.

What Is Calcium?

Calcium is a mineral, but it does not exist alone in nature. Calcium attaches to a chemical saltlike carbonate or phosphate to form a calcium salt. Calcium salts and therefore calcium exist in abundance in nature.

three glasses of milk? You do not ordinarily see people belly up to a bar and order a glass of milk. Or how about a glass of milk with that steak?

Of all the calcium in the human body, 99 percent is found in the bones. Bone is not synonymous with calcium, but it might as well be. In the bones, calcium and phosphorus combine to form a crystalline structure called hydroxyapatite, which gives the bone strength. The other one percent of the calcium in our body circulates in the blood. Although calcium is essential for bone health, it is also necessary for the heart, muscles, and nerves to work. In addition, calcium plays a major role in getting blood to clot, as when we cut ourselves. An individual loses calcium through their urine, feces, and sweat and

1994 National Institutes of Health (NIH) Recommendations for Daily Calcium Intake

Group	Recommended Calcium Intake in Milligrams
Infants	
Birth–6 months	400
6 months–1 year	600
Children	
1–5 years	800
6–10 years	800–1,200
Adolescents/Young Adults	
11–24 years	1,200–1,500
Men	
25–65 years	1,000
Over 65 years	1,500
Women	
25–50 years	1,000
Over 50 years (or postmenopausal)	
Taking ERT/HRT	1,000
Not taking ERT/HRT	1,500
Over 65 years regardless of ERT/HRT	1,500
Pregnant or nursing	1,200–1,500

when they shed skin, hair, and nails. We replace this calcium with foods in our diet or supplements. But there is more to proper calcium balance and maintaining healthy bones than just calcium intake. Other dietary factors affect absorption and excretion or loss of calcium. Vitamin D is crucial to calcium absorption. Proteins are essential to build tissue during growth and repair, such as fracture healing. However, when the body consumes protein, the products that are excreted by the body to break down the protein increase calcium loss. Table salt, which contains sodium and chloride, also increases calcium loss.

So how much calcium is enough? The amount differs as an individual ages, but there is never an age when we do not need calcium. The stage of life, pregnant or not, nursing, on ERT or HRT, and other factors dictates the recommended requirements.

Individuals cannot manufacture calcium, they must consume it. If an individual does not consume enough calcium, the body is forced to remove calcium from the bones and give it to the blood, robbing the bones of the calcium that makes them strong. The solution, of course, is to be sure that the body never has a reason to take calcium out of the bone.

In 1995, a summary of thirty-one research studies that looked at the relationship between bone density and calcium in women between the ages of eighteen and fifty concluded that calcium supplementation of 1,000mg a day in this age group would prevent bone loss. (See 1994 National Institutes of Health (NIH) Recommendations for Daily Calcium Intake to know exactly how much supplementation is needed.) Taking calcium now will reduce the risk of bone fracture later.

Osteoporactic fractures occur because the skeleton becomes so fragile that the bone breaks. This fragility, or lack of density, is the sum of two things: how dense the bones were when they were at their peak and how much bone loss has been experienced since that time. Calcium plays a role in both.

Many experts believe that osteoporosis is really a disease that begins in childhood. Perhaps 80 percent of bone density is genetically determined; the other 20 percent is up to the individual. For a growing child, receiving the recommended amount of calcium helps the bones reach their peak density as predetermined by heredity. The greater the peak bone density, the more

Calcium Content of Dairy Products

Dairy Group	Serving Size	Milligrams of Calcium Per Serving
Milk		
Whole	1 cup	291
2%	1 cup	297
1%	1 cup	300
Skim	1 cup	302
Buttermilk	1 cup	285
Yogurt		
Low fat	1 cup	415
Frozen	1 cup	240
Fat-free frozen	1 cup	224
Cheese		
Ricotta	½ cup	337
Swiss	1oz	272
Monterey Jack	1oz	212
Mozzarella, skim	1oz	207
Cheddar	1oz	204
Colby	1oz	194
American	1oz	174
Ice Cream (11 Percent Fat)		
Regular	1 cup	176
Soft Serve	1 cup	236

Calcium Content of Some Nondairy Foods

Food Group	Serving Size	Milligrams of Calcium Per Serving
Seafood		
Sardines with bones	3oz	372
Oysters	1 cup	226
Fried Shrimp, batter dipped	3.5oz	72
Red Snapper	3.5oz	16
Vegetables		
Fresh Collards, cooked	1 cup	357
Fresh Turnip Greens, cooked	1 cup	252
Okra	½ cup	88
Green Beans, frozen	½ cup	31
Raw Cauliflower	1 cup	25
Fruits and Nuts		
Almonds	¼ cup	94
Brazil Nuts	¼ cup	62
Meats/Protein		
Egg, hard boiled	1 egg	28

(continued)

Pork Sausage, smoked	1 link	20
Grains/Breads		
7" Waffle	1	179
4" Pancakes	2	72
White Bread	1 slice	32

loss it will take before the bones become fragile enough to break.

In 1992, researchers at the University of Indiana followed seventy pairs of identical twins six to fourteen years of age. One twin was given a calcium supplement while the other was given a placebo for three years. Both twins obviously had the same genetic potential, but calcium supplementation resulted in a 5.1 percent greater bone density in the wrist and a 2.8 percent greater bone density in the spine.

The easiest source of calcium is a dairy product, but there are also fortified juices and beverages. Some brands of bread and rice are also calcium fortified.

While it is important to include foods that contain calcium in a daily diet, calcium supplements can be an efficient way to get the necessary calcium. I take a calcium supplement every day and I have for years. I take 500mg in the morning and 500mg at night.

Calcium tablets are large because calcium salts are big in size. The higher the amount of calcium in a tablet the larger it is going to be. The most important aspect of choosing a calcium supplement is to make sure that it meets the United States Pharmacopeia (USP) standards. The container's label will indicate if the tablets are USP approved.

Calcium supplements should be taken with meals to help in the absorption process. Calcium citrate, however, can be taken on an empty stomach. Also, this supplement is good for individuals who might have a history of kidney stones.

Calcium supplements may be swallowed or chewed. There are chocolate and caramel-coated calcium supplements. There are even brands that work like Tums. A partial list of common calcium supplements follows. There are hundreds of brands available in drugstores, groceries, and health-food stores.

Common Calcium Supplements

Calcium Carbonate
Caltrate 600 (multiple products)
Nature-Made Calcium
Oscal 500 (multiple products)
Osteo-CAL
TUMS 500 Calcium Supplement
Viactiv Soft Calcium Chews

Calcium Citrate
Centrum Focused Formulas Bone
    Health
Citracal (multiple products)

Calcium Phosphate
Milk Calcium 700 with Vitamins
    C & D
Posture-D

Mixed Calcium Carbonate, Phosphate, and Citrate
Nature's Reward CalciComplex
    Advanced Formula

Mixed Calcium Gluconate, Lactate, and Carbonate
Calcet

How Much Calcium Does an Individual Need Every Day?

To determine how much calcium should be consumed every day, look at the table on page 128 to see the recommended doses for age and circumstance. Assume 500mg comes from food, without counting any milk. Drinking milk every day adds 300mg of calcium for every glass. Now how does this compare to the amount the table says is necessary? Are you still short? If you are, you must increase your dairy product consumption and/or add a calcium-fortified beverage or food. Taking a calcium supplement is also an option. Determine how many tablets of the supplement are necessary to meet the recommended calcium intake. Take the supplement with meals, and if it is necessary to take more than one tablet a day, split them up. There is no added benefit to taking more calcium than necessary.

Vitamin D

In order to prevent osteoporosis, everyone needs to take vitamin D along with calcium since this helps in absorption.

Vitamin D can be found in a limited number of foods and beverages. That old standard, cod liver oil, is loaded with vitamin D. Most milk in the U.S. is fortified with vitamin D. (Do not be fooled — even though milk is fortified with vitamin D, not all dairy products contain vitamin D, so be sure to check the nutrition label.) The sun is also important. Exposure to sunlight can help your body manufacture vitamin D, although the time of year and the amount (if any) of sunblock used will dictate the amount of vitamin D produced.

Vitamin K

Vitamin K has received a lot of attention in the last few years for its potential role in osteoporosis. Vitamin K1, which is what humans need, is found in lettuce, cabbage, green beans, and cauliflower. It is also found in pigs' and calves' liver. Virtually all multivitamins will contain vitamin K although they may not contain as much as an individual needs. The suggested daily

National Academy of Science Dietary Reference Daily Intake Values for Vitamin D	
Age	*Adequate Intake (AI) in International Units (IU)*
Birth–50 years	200
51–70 years	400
71+	600

There is no increase in the AI for vitamin D for pregnant or nursing women up to age fifty.

consumption of vitamin K is 75mg for girls fourteen to eighteen and 90mg for women nineteen and older. One cup of lettuce contains 95mg of vitamin K. Stop whining and eat your salad.

Prescription Medications

With all the vitamins and the prescription medicine I take daily and the amount of traveling I do, you might imagine I would lose track of what I need to take, but I have a system. I keep my vitamins and medication in a fishing-tackle box. Not one of the big ones that comes with a collapsible lid, but a plastic container divided into sections. It is easy to work with on my bathroom counter, and that way I can remember everything I need to take by filling up the slots. I take the tackle box with me when I travel. It is a joy to live in a time when we have medicine that helps keep us stable and pain free. When we look at the way our grandmothers and our mothers suffered, we have to realize how fortunate we are to have medications available to prevent or arrest osteoporosis.

The medications presently available in the treatment of osteoporosis are: Miacalcin Nasal Spray; Fosamax (both in a daily and weekly form); Actonel (also available in daily and weekly form); Evista and Forteo. With the exception of Forteo, which builds bone and helps stop bone loss, Miacalcin, Fosamax, Actonal, and Evista are called antiresorptives. In Chapter 4 Dr. Levine explained how bone is remodeled in two stages. In the first stage of bone resorption, bone tissue is dissolved and small cavities are created. In the second stage, new bone fills the cavities. Anti-resorptives slow the resorption of bone, but do not build new bone. Genericbrands of antiosteoporosis medications are not available at this time, but may be in the future. The following are the brand names and their scientific names for reference:

Actonel	Risedronate
Evista	Raloxifene
Forteo	Teriparatide
Fosamax	Alendronate
Miacalcin	Calcitonin

I tried most of these medications before I found what works for me. I am a believer in Evista. I have taken Evista for four years and I am a spokesperson for Eli Lilly, which owns the patent for Evista. Dr. Levine has been a member of the speakers' bureau for Eli Lilly.

Miacalcin Nasal Spray

The first medication prescribed by my doctor was Miacalcin Nasal Spray, which is the same synthetic salmon calcitonin originally approved by the FDA for the treatment of osteoporosis in postmenopausal women. Calcitonin will reduce the risk of spine fracture, although to date has not been shown to reduce the risk of nonspinal fractures.

Miacalcin is officially approved by the FDA for the treatment of women who are postmenopausal for at least five years and

Salmon?

A bone hormone, calcitonin, is manufactured in the thyroid. It is not a thyroid hormone — it is simply made in the same gland. Other species manufacture this hormone, including salmon. It is the synthetic version of salmon calcitonin that was originally used in the treatment of osteoporosis in an injectable form and is now available as a nasal spray.

No one has ever been able to prove that a deficiency of calcitonin causes postmenopausal osteoporosis. Nevertheless salmon calcitonin treatment of postmenopausal women with osteoporosis results in a slowing or stopping of bone loss in the spine. In 1984, the FDA approved synthetic salmon calcitonin for women who were at least five years postmenopausal. Salmon calcitonin was used because it is more potent than human calcitonin. At that time, it was available only by injection. The injections were fairly painless, but they were expensive and few people wanted to take

(continued)

a medication requiring a shot every day. In 1995, things got a lot easier with the introduction of synthetic salmon calcitonin in the form of a nasal spray.

The injectable form of salmon calcitonin is still available by prescription, although it is not used a great deal today. In addition to stopping bone loss, one of the potential benefits of salmon-calcitonin treatment is relief of pain from a fracture. Salmon calcitonin was never approved for the relief of pain, but there are reports in medical literature that women who had acute fractures in their spine obtained significant and rapid pain relief when given salmon-calcitonin injections.

Fosamax

The first study on Fosamax, conducted in 1995, was called a Fracture Intervention Trial (FIT). This study of the effectiveness of Fosamax for the treatment of osteoporosis in many ways set the standard for research in this field.

(Continued)

Over 26,000 women were deemed eligible to participate. The women had to be at least two years postmenopausal and between the ages of fifty-five and eighty-one. They also had to have a low bone density in the hip. They were divided into two groups, depending on whether they had had a spine fracture or not.

At the end of this three-year study, the women with a prior spine fracture who received Fosamax instead of a placebo had marked increases in the bone density in their spine and hip. Even more dramatic was the finding that Fosamax reduced the risk of future spine fractures by 47 percent and the risk for future hip fractures by 51 percent. The results from the second group were just as impressive.

In both arms of the trial the dose of Fosamax was one 5mg tablet a day for the first two years of the study. The dose was increased to one 10mg tablet a day in the third year because of findings from other studies, which showed that the 10mg dose resulted in greater gains in bone density.

Researchers were also interested in

(continued)

whether Fosamax could be used to prevent bone loss in recently postmenopausal women not taking estrogen replacement. This study had 447 women in it. They were forty to fifty-nine years of age and not more than three years postmenopausal. At the end of the three years, the women who took at least 5mg of Fosamax a day maintained the bone density in their spines and hips.

Actonel

The generic name of Actonel is risedronate. In the North American Vetebral Efficacy with Risedronate Therapy (VERT) trial, 2,458 postmenopausal women under the age of eighty-five who had at least one spine fracture took either a placebo or 5mg of Actonel once a day. All of the women received a calcium supplement. At the end of three years, the women who took 5mg of Actonel had a 41 percent reduction in the risk of new spine fractures. Their spine bone density was 4.3 percent better than that of the women who had taken a placebo and 2.8 percent better at the hip.

Another study of Actonel, called HIP,
(continued)

was conducted to evaluate the effectiveness of Actonel in reducing the risk of hip fracture in postmenopausal women. "HIP" stands for Hip Intervention Program. The study involved over 5,000 women age seventy and older. At the end of the three-year study, women who had taken Actonel had a lower risk of hip fracture than the women who had taken a placebo.

The effects of Actonel in preventing bone loss in healthy, postmenopausal women has also been studied. In a two-year study of women with an average age of fifty-three who were three years postmenopausal or less, bone density in the spine and hip increased in the women taking Actonel while women taking a placebo lost bone density. In another study of slightly older women with low bone density but no fractures, 5mg of Actonel a day resulted in increases in spine and hipbone density compared to women taking a placebo.

The dose of Actonel that was effective in these studies for either the treatment of osteoporosis or the prevention (continued) was one 5mg tablet a day. Unlike Fosamax, the dose for prevention is the same as the dose for treatment. Actonel is taken exactly like Fosamax.

In May 2002, a once-a-week dose of Actonel was approved by the FDA.

Does Fosamax Have Adverse Effects?

A key issue is whether digestive problems occur with Fosamax or Actonel. There has been a great deal of interest in comparing Fosamax and Actonel to determine if either medication is safer than the other.

In the studies involving both drugs, literally thousands of women have had their complaints recorded in meticulous detail. If a woman complains of a headache, this is recorded. If she develops a cold, this is recorded. And if she complains of indigestion, this is recorded. It
(continued)

does not matter if the researcher thinks the complaint is related to the drug or not. With rare exceptions, the researcher does not know if the woman is taking a placebo or the real drug. At the end of the study, the "adverse events" as these complaints are called are totaled. Then the researchers look at the percentage of women with any type of complaint and compare the number of women taking the drug who developed the complaint to the number of women taking a placebo with the same complaint. Only then can it really be determined whether the drug appears to cause the problem or not.

With Fosamax, the most common digestive symptom has been stomach pain. In two studies from Europe and the United States that involved 590 women, abdominal pain was a complaint in 6.6 percent of the women taking Fosamax. It was also a complaint in 4.8 percent of women taking a placebo.

Other digestive complaints that have been noted in the many Fosamax
(continued)

studies include nausea, constipation, diarrhea, heartburn, and indigestion. The percentage of women taking Fosamax experiencing these complaints is less than 4 percent. And the percentage of women taking a placebo with these same complaints is virtually identical. The same thing is true for Actonel.

As with any concern about medication or its side effects, talk to your doctor.

have a low bone mass in comparison with healthy premenopausal women. I tried Miacalcin for a while, but found that since I am on the road a lot and live in two different places, it was hard to keep up with a medication that had to be stored in a cool place. And because it is a pump spray, I never could tell whether I was actually getting the appropriate dose. Directions call for one squeeze a day in the nose alternating nostrils daily. Sometimes it seemed like I was getting a lot and sometimes it did not seem like I was getting any medicine at all, so I told my doctor that I did not like the spray and he prescribed another medication called Fosamax.

Fosamax and Actonel (The bisphosphanates)

When I took Fosamax I had to take it every day and there were a lot of instructions about when to take it and how. Fosamax has to be taken first thing in the morning before drinking or eating anything. It must be taken with a full glass of water. And then for thirty minutes after taking the medicine there is still no eating or drinking, nor lying back down. When I am up, I want coffee. And it was impossible to time it when I was out of town in a hotel and someone was waiting downstairs for a breakfast meeting. I took 10mg of Fosamax once a day, which is the dose recommended for treatment of postmenopausal osteoporosis. The recommended dose for prevention of postmenopausal osteoporosis is 5mg a day.

Although the instructions are the same, now that Fosamax is available in a dose that is taken once a week, it makes it much easier to fit into a routine. If taken once a week the doses should be 35mg if prevention is the goal, and a 70mg tablet for treatment of osteoporosis; same instructions for both. Dr. Levine says the greatest gains in bone density (using Fosamax) are in the first few years of use, but in studies of women who have taken Fosamax continuously for up to seven years, additional small gains in bone density have been seen every year. Fosamax is approved by the FDA for the treatment and prevention of postmenopausal osteoporosis. Also, Fosamax is approved for the treatment of osteoporosis in men. I never took Actonel, but I understand that it is similar to Fosamax, and also can be taken in a once-a-week tablet.

So how long should one take either Actonel or Fosamax? There are various recommendations, because the drugs sit in the bone for a long time and consequently have a residual effect even after being stopped. Bone density does fall when either is stopped, but at a much slower rate. Some say to reevaluate after five years, but under any circumstances it is important to have a repeat bone-density test a year after stopping either medication.

Evista

It is important to note that my doctor worked with me until we found the right medication. I did not lose patience, nor did he. We communicated about what was not working for me and why. Sure enough, the right medication became available. My doctor told me that there was a new drug coming out that I was going to like because I only had to take it once a day and it did not matter if I had eaten or not.

Evista is a totally different medication from Miacalcin, Fosamax, or Actonel. Evista belongs to a family of medications called Selective Estrogen Receptor Modulators, or SERMs. SERMs are a class of medications that have deliberately been designed to mimic some of the beneficial ac-

---

MORE — In 1999 the findings from the Multiple Outcomes of Raloxifene Evaluation Trial of Evista's ability to reduce the risk of spine fracture in postmenopausal women with osteoporosis were reported in the *Journal of the American Medical Association*. More than 7,000 postmenopausal women up to eighty years of age participated in the MORE trial. *At the end of the three-year trial, the women who were taking one 60mg tablet a day of Evista had a 30 percent reduction in their risk of spine fractures compared to women taking a placebo. They also had spine and hipbone densities that were 2.6 percent and 2.1 percent better than those of the women taking a placebo.*

---

tions of estrogen. In lay terms, Evista is a designer drug that mimics estrogen's effect on bones while acting in an opposite fashion on the breasts and uterus. Consequently, unlike HRTs, it does not cause uterine bleeding or stimulate the growth of breast tissue. In clinical trials of Evista, the thickness of the uterus lining was measured with a technique called transvaginal ultrasonography, and there was no significant difference in the thicknesses measured in the women taking a placebo compared to the women taking Evista. Other studies have shown that Evista does not increase the risk of uterine cancer. Vaginal bleeding while taking Evista must be reported to your doctor.

As for breast cancer risk, Evista does not appear to increase it. In fact, in one trial, four years of Evista was associated with a 72-percent *reduction* in the risk of invasive breast cancer. However, it is not FDA approved for breast cancer prevention. Besides helping to counteract bone loss, Evista can help with cholesterol levels.

Evista mimics estrogen in both positive and negative outcomes. One of the risks is that Evista can increase the possibility of blood clots especially when you are not able to move for hours at a time. I stop taking Evista seventy-two hours before a long plane or car ride. It should also be stopped before surgery or when bed rest is prescribed. I fly so much that if there is any danger of blood clots I try to minimize it. And I do not notice any change in the way I feel when I stop taking Evista for a few days. Evista should not be restarted until normal activity has been resumed. Evista should not be taken with HRTs.

It would be nice if Evista reduced hot flashes, but it does not lessen the occurrence of these. The most common complaint attributed to Evista is leg cramps, but in most cases, these complaints were mild and did not result in the women stopping Evista.

Officially, Evista is indicated for the prevention and treatment of postmenopausal osteoporosis in a dose of one 60mg tablet once a day. It can be taken any time of the day. Evista should not be taken by women who are pregnant or who may become pregnant or by women who are breast-feeding. It should also not be taken by women who have or have had problems with blood clots in the legs, pelvis, lungs, or eyes. Women taking estrogen should not take Evista.

Forteo, or teriparatidfe, is the newest medication for treating severe osteoporosis. A form of parathyroid hormone, it must be administered in a daily injection and is used for two years only. Forteo differs from the antiresorptives because it stimulates new bone formation which is reflected in increased bone density. Studies reveal that Forteo lowers the risk of spinal fractures by 65 percent and nonspinal fractures by 53 percent when compared to a placebo. There is a warning about increased risk for osteosarcoma (cancer of the bone), so each woman should consult carefully with her own doctor to see if Forteo is right for her.

WHO SHOULD TAKE OSTEOPOROSIS PREVENTION MEDICINES?

The question of who should take medications like Miacalcin, Evista, Actonel, or Fosamax is touched on in Chapter 3: Getting a Bone-Density Test. Several major medical organizations have published guidelines, but they are only guidelines and should not be substituted for discussion with your physician.

The guidelines all refer to the T-score Chart in Chapter 3. A T-score of 0 means that the bone density is exactly the same as the average bone density for a young adult. A T-score greater than 0 means that the bone density is higher than the average bone density of the young adult. A T-score of 0 or above is considered great. A T-score down to -1 is still considered normal. When the T-score falls below -1, careful consideration and a discussion with your doctor to determine what is best for you is warranted.

Guidelines

- The National Ostcoporosis Foundation (NOF) published guidelines in 1998. It recommends prescription therapy be considered in a postmenopausal woman if her bone density is below a T-score of -2. She should consider therapy if her bone density is only below a -1.5 if she has any other risk factor for osteoporosis (see lists of risk factors, Chapter 4). Elderly women might have so many nonbone-density risk factors that treatment should be considered regardless of bone density.

- The American Association of Clinical Endocrinologists (AACE) published guidelines in 2001. It recommends that prescription medication be considered for postmenopausal women who have T-scores of -2.5 or lower. If risk factors are present, a T-score of -1.5 or lower justifies treatment. AACE also recommends treatment if a woman has any degree of low-bone density plus a fracture.
- The North American Menopause Society (NAMS) published guidelines in 2002. NAMS recommends that postmenopausal women with either a spine or hip T-score poorer than -2.5 consider medication. If a woman has a spine or hip T-score of -2.0 to -2.5 she should still consider therapy if she has any additional risk factors. Finally, if a postmenopausal woman has already had a fracture, she should consider therapy regardless of bone density.

Though there are slight differences in these guidelines, they all recognize that osteoporosis is a preventable and treatable disease and that medications are available now to help do just that. A woman and her physician need to determine her risk for osteoporosis and fracture and make a choice based on that information. They should keep working together until she finds the right medication regimen.

Kids and Their Bones

Osteoporosis has been called a pediatric disease with geriatric consequences, because the bone mass attained in childhood and adolescence is crucial to the lifelong health of the bones. The health habits formed as a kid can make or break bones as they age. Following are tips from the National Institutes of Health:

- Be a role model. Drink milk with meals, eat calcium-rich snacks, and get plenty of weight-bearing exercise. Do not smoke.
- Incorporate calcium-rich foods into family meals.
- Serve fat-free or lowfat milk with meals and snacks.
- Stock up on calcium-rich snacks that are easy for hungry children to find, such as cheese cubes and string cheese, calcium-fortified orange juice, single-serving puddings, individual cheese pizzas, yogurt and frozen yo-

gurt, tortillas, cereal with lowfat milk, almonds, and broccoli with yogurt dip.

- Limit access to soft drinks and other snacks that do not provide calcium, by not keeping them in the house.
- Help your kids find a variety of physical activities or sports they enjoy participating in.
- Establish a firm time limit for sedentary activities such as watching TV, using computers, and playing video games.
- Teach your kids to never start smoking, as it is highly addictive and toxic.
- Look for signs of eating disorders and overtraining, especially in preteen and teenage girls, and address these problems right away.
- Talk to your children's pediatrician about their bone health. If your child has a special medical condition that may interfere with bone mass development, ask the doctor to minimize the problem and protect your child's bone health.
- Talk to your children about their bone health, and let them know it is a priority for you. Your kids may not think

much about health, but they are probably attracted to such health benefits as energy, confidence, good looks, and strength.

CHAPTER 8

EXERCISE

If anyone had told me that when I reached my sixth decade I would begin lifting free weights and working out on weight-training machinery, I would have called them crazy.

When I was young, no one knew the importance of exercise for girls. We ran only because we needed to get from here to there and our feet were our transportation. At the little Lakeview country school, we got to play basketball because that was literally the only thing to do. Girls were allowed to play only on one half of the court, so if you were playing defense and you could get the ball away from the other team, you could dribble to midcourt but then you had to pass it to one of your teammates on the other side of the line. My team was called the Lakeview Bulldogs. We actually got uniforms and this was a big deal for a little country school. One game, I had my new uniform on and I was up for a free throw. A boy I had been admiring for a long time shouted out at me, "Make that basket, Bird Legs!" I was totally crushed, but it was true. I had skinny legs. I was skinny then, though I quit being "bird legs" about forty pounds ago.

When I got to Baylor University, women could bowl for P.E. class. I loved bowling because I did not have to change clothes like I had to for gym class. Women could also take calisthenics, but after sophomore year women did not have to participate in any other physical activity. Title IX has improved women's sports. Now, schools are mandated to provide money for girls' competitive sports at the same level as for boys'. I sincerely hope that one of the benefits of Title IX funds is that as the girls of the future grow up to be women, their bones will not be as vulnerable to fracture as the bones of my generation. I think Title IX is one of the most important advances for young women in my lifetime.

The potential benefits of exercise at any age are far-reaching. Exercise helps the heart and lowers blood pressure. It lowers cholesterol and boosts the immune system. It alleviates depression and reduces the risk of falling. It increases strength and agility. What exercise can do for bones depends in part on the age of the individual. For children, adolescents, and young adults, regular exercise will help build bone density. For a mature adult, exercise helps to maintain bone density by preventing bone loss. Exercise can also improve balance and agility to reduce the risk of falling. Even a woman who already has severe osteoporosis can benefit from the right kind of exercise.

Since I was diagnosed with osteopenia, I have exercised regularly. Actually, even before I became aware of the benefits of weight-bearing exercise, I had started walking on a regular basis with my dear friend Virginia Whitten. Virginia and I had just stopped smoking and somewhere we had heard that exercise would help reduce the craving for cigarettes.

Austin has a beautiful lake, Town Lake, with a six-mile loop. It is one of the very best walking trails anywhere in the country. Virginia and I walked half of the six-mile loop. We started our walks shortly after Virginia found out she had breast cancer. One day we were walking along, and she veered off to the left. The first time it happened, we did not think anything about it. But the next time, she said,

"I think something is wrong." Later, she found out that the reason she was having problems walking in a straight line was that the breast cancer had metastasized to her spinal fluid, which affected her balance. She died about five years later. I miss Virginia. She was such a good friend and our walks were a wonderful way to spend time together.

The last few years, I have been walking with my daughter, Ellen. We do the same three-mile route I walked with Virginia. Ellen and I finish the walk in forty to forty-five minutes. I cherish this time spent with Ellen. Now that I live part-time in New York City, I walk even more. I walk everywhere in the city.

If we do not exercise, our bones do not become strong or stay strong. Bone responds in a very specific way to physical forces. Bone becomes more dense in response to physical force and less dense when we are sedentary.

Although I had been walking for years, I did not go to the gym. I was doing a lot of flying and I was beginning to feel like I had been folded up and stuffed in an envelope. Flying is hard on the body and I have a couple of bad disks in my back, so by the time I get off an airplane, I am really stiff.

Walking Helps Prevent Osteoporosis

To benefit the bones, exercise must be either weight-bearing or strength-training in nature. Weight-bearing exercise is any type of exercise in which the bones must support the body weight against gravity. Walking is weight-bearing because the body has to hold itself upright. Other types of weight-bearing activities are baseball, basketball, tennis, and volleyball. Swimming is not a weight-bearing activity because the water bears the body's weight. A one-year study of 239 healthy postmenopausal women found that walking only one mile each day was enough to make the bone density at the spine better, compared with that of women who walked shorter distances. In this study, the women walked on their own without going to a gym or a track.

After one trip, I called my assistant and said, "I feel terrible. See if you can find someone to come to my house and give me a massage."

A young masseuse named Debra Snell arrived the next day. I was telling her about my osteopenia and she said, "One of the things that could really help is exercise. I am a trainer, and I want you to come to my gym in the morning."

The thought of lifting weights was ridiculous to me, so I said, "Well, I am not going to do that." And then, of course, the

Doing the Moon Walk

The ultimate test for ascertaining the effects of weight-bearing activity on bones occurred in space, where there is zero gravity. In the early phases of the space program, Gemini and Apollo astronauts underwent bone-density measurements before and after space missions. These early flights were four to fourteen days long; nevertheless postflight bone-density tests showed significant loss of density.

more I thought about it, the more I realized there was no way I could afford not to try it. That was the beginning of my weight-lifting program.

It was my walking dates with Virginia that taught me how another person can motivate you to exercise. After she was ill, I thought I was walking for Virginia because on our walks she got a chance to talk about her feelings at this difficult time of her life, but in reality, I was doing it for myself. No matter how busy I was, or how grumpy I felt about taking my walk, I had to be there for Virginia. That is how I learned that if you have an appointment you will not disappoint the person who is waiting for you. Part of the reason I work with a personal trainer is because I have to show up! If I have made an appointment, I will be there. Also, working with Debra helped me make good choices about my diet. Being around someone who is health conscious makes a lot of difference in our own behavior.

I think in some ways Debra saved my life. She gave me a sense of self-confidence about working out and taught me the value of exercise. She helped me see the difference in how exercise makes me feel about my own ability to care for myself, avoid injury, and be strong enough to do anything I want to do.

It is not always easy to find time to exercise, but it is essential. It is easy to find an excuse not to exercise. We say we are too busy or we worked hard all day. I suppose we think we can squeak by without exercising regularly, not realizing that health, stamina, and our sense of well-being are gradually declining. We rationalize by thinking, "Well, I am not as young as I used to be."

I give speeches about osteoporosis and the need to take care of our health. Invariably women will come up to me after the speech and express concern about finding the time to exercise or whether or not lifting weights will give them bulging muscles or take up too much time. The exercise needed to maintain good health will not cause bulging muscles. Just look at celebrities like Madonna and Cameron Diaz. They look beautiful and healthy. They seem to glow. I attribute that glow to working out. If going to a gym is not an option, exercising at home is just as effective. But putting exercise off by saying that it is too expensive or takes too much time is really a conscious decision not to exercise.

My number one priority is to get to the gym twice a week. Number two is to try to walk six to nine miles a week. At the gym I work my muscles until they are fatigued, which activates, regenerates, and rebuilds them. I do not go to a gym every day because my muscles need time to rest.

There are many different exercises that can help bones. I love free weights, but I also use the weight-training machines. My trainers vary the way I work out so that I do not get bored.

GLOSSARY OF KEY EXERCISE TERMS

Aerobic — Exercises that cause the muscles to move in a continuous rhythmic fashion. Most exercises that end in "-ing" are aerobic. Jogging, swimming, running, bicycling. Bear in mind that not all aerobic activities are weight-bearing. To be considered a weight-bearing exercise, the body must support its own weight during the exercise.

Anaerobic — Brief but strenuous exercise. Exercise using weight-training machines and free weights is anaerobic.

Barbells — A bar with weights attached to each end. To increase the weight, more weights are added to each side.

168

How Much Exercise?

The amount of exercise an individual needs to affect bone density is partially determined by age. Studies of weight-bearing and strength-training exercise in children have proven that the younger the child begins and the longer she continues, the greater the benefit to her bones. Girls who participate in routine weight-bearing activities develop higher peak bone densities than girls who do not. Stronger bones in a girl means more prevention against osteoporosis when she is mature.

In a study conducted by the Washington University School of Medicine, thirty-five postmenopausal women ages fifty-five to seventy walked or jogged on a treadmill or used a stair-climbing machine three times a week. After only nine months the mineral content in the spine of these women had increased an average of 5.2%. After twenty-two months, the mineral content had increased 6.1%.

Circuits — Refers to a group of exercise machines. In a gym, the machines used for one's individual exercise program make up a circuit.

Dumbbell — A free weight that has weights permanently fixed to both ends of a short bar. Different dumbbells are used for different weights.

Free Weights — Hand-held or wrap-around devices that weigh specific amounts such as five pounds, ten pounds, etc. When one is "doing free weights" one is lifting the devices, usually one in each hand, in a movement meant to exercise a specific group of muscles.

Impact Loading — Refers to exercise that transmits force through the bones. Jumping rope and tennis are two examples. Impact-loading exercise is not good for women who already have osteopenia or osteoporosis, but this type of exercise is excellent for preventing bone loss in one's younger years.

Reps — Short for repetitions. One rep refers to lifting or, in the case of machines, pushing a weight one time. Each push or pull on the weight is a rep. Eight reps means the weight has been lifted eight times.

Spine Extension Exercises — Refers to movements that "open up" the back and spine. Recommended for women with osteoporosis.

Spine Flexion — Also called trunk flexion. This refers to the movement of bending forward from the waist with the back rounded. Old-fashioned sit-ups put the spine into flexion. *Spine flexion has the potential to injure the spine.*

Before starting any exercise program you should talk to your doctor. There are many exercises to choose from, and exercise programs for each person may vary. Consulting your doctor will help you decide which program is best for you. For example, I do many of the exercises shown here, but Dr. Levine has included other good exercises. *No person over the age of forty should exercise without consulting a physician.*

GENERAL RECOMMENDATIONS FOR EXERCISE PROGRAMS

- For each exercise session, choose either aerobic or anaerobic exercise. For

171

example, do aerobic weight-bearing exercise one day (for instance, walking on Monday). The next exercise session can then be devoted to strength training (for instance, free weights on Tuesday).

- Give yourself at least forty-eight hours between strength-training sessions.
- Do not try to lift so much weight that you cannot do at least eight reps with good form. Work up to at least ten reps before increasing the weight. Go slow, especially during the first eight weeks.
- When using either free weights or

Stretching

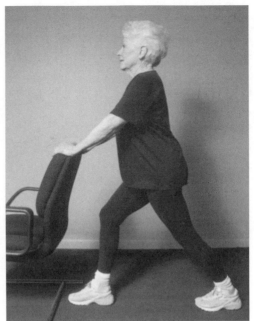

Stretching

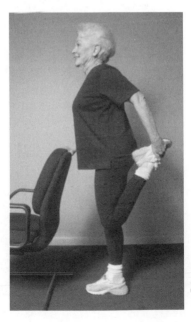

Stretching

strength-training machines, it is imperative that the spine is straight or even slightly arched. If you are using a machine, the height of the seat should be adjusted so that you can place both feet on the floor while keeping your back against the backrest. If you must reach with your arms during the exercise, the seat should be moved or the arm levers adjusted so that you can keep your back straight during the exercise. If the machine cannot be adjusted to fit, do not use it.

• Stretching exercises should be performed at least three times a week. There are three different types of stretching, but static stretching is really the safest and most effective. In static stretching, you slowly stretch the muscle until you feel mild discomfort and hold the stretch for ten to thirty seconds. Then slowly release the stretch. Deep breathing during the stretch promotes further relaxation of the stretched muscle and allows you to extend the stretch.

• Do not stretch cold. Perform a gentle activity, like walking, to warm up before stretching or lifting weights.

• A workout should not exceed one

hour and that includes ten minutes of stretching and a cool-down period.

THE EXERCISES ARE DIVIDED INTO TWO SECTIONS:

1. Exercises to prevent bone loss and strengthen muscle. These are exercises for anyone who has not lost significant bone, and who is concerned about maintaining bone density and increasing muscle strength.
2. Exercises for women with osteoporosis.

1. Exercises to Prevent Bone Loss and Strengthen Muscle

Exercising when we are younger helps to build bone density. After thirty, peak bone density has been achieved, but continuing to exercise is important to maintain bone density. This is true whether you are a premenopausal or postmenopausal woman. There is no upper age limit at which exercise is not beneficial — studies on people over the age of ninety have shown that exercise improves strength and agility and in some cases has even reversed poor physical condition caused by years of inactivity!

Strength-training exercises are designed to exercise specific muscles or groups of muscles. To exercise all of the muscle groups, different exercises are needed. For the prevention of osteoporosis, the most important areas are the back, hips, upper legs, shoulders, and arms. For each area, exercise machines or free weights can be used, depending on which you prefer.

One set of the maximum weight that you can comfortably lift, at eight to ten repetitions, will be sufficient. However, you may do up to three sets by either repeating the exercise for a muscle group or rotating to a different group. Good form is very important to avoid injury and strain.

Finding your maximum weight for each exercise is a matter of trial and error. If you belong to a gym, you should consult with a certified trainer who will be able to observe your form with each exercise and record the weight you used. Make sure you know how to use the weights and machinery at a gym properly and safely. For each exercise I have included exercises to be done at the gym on machines and alternatives to be done using free weights at home. The same rules apply for doing exercises at home: Be sure you choose weights you are very comfortable with and be sure to keep your posture symmetrical. Even for home exercises, consultation and periodic reevaluation with a certified trainer or physical therapist is recommended.

Remember to rest between each exercise and to always return the weight to its original position slowly. Make sure you breathe while you exercise. I exhale on the exertion.

EXERCISES FOR THE BACK

The back extension — In the gym, using a back-extension resistance machine, sit on the saddle leaning back against the padded bar (the bar should come across the back just below the shoulder blades). Push back against the bar, raising the stack of weights. You can perform the same exercise at home by lying on the floor face-down, arms at your sides, and placing a firm pillow under your hips to decrease stress on the lower back. Lift your head and shoulders off the floor. Hold for three counts. When you have mastered this, you can increase the difficulty by lifting your feet off the floor at the same time. Five repetitions for this exercise should suffice.

EXERCISES FOR THE SHOULDERS, UPPER ARMS, UPPER AND MIDDLE BACK

The lat pull-down — In the gym, sit under the bar, grasp the bar with an overhand grip (your hands should be placed on the bar farther apart than the width of your shoulders). Sit up straight. Pull the bar down in front of your head to chest level. As you pull the bar down in front, the

Lat pull-down

upper chest muscles are working harder.

At home you can sit in a firm chair toward the front of the seat with feet flat on the floor. Lift yourself by pushing down on the hands, raising your trunk and buttocks off the seat. Hold for the count of three. Do not push down with your feet and legs, and be sure that you do not shrug your shoulders.

The bent-over row — In the gym or at home this exercise uses free weights. Place your feet comfortably apart, bend at the waist (do not round your back!) and lift the weight straight up so that your elbow bends above the back. Keep your knees slightly bent during the exercise. I like to

Bent-over row

put my knee on a bench as in the photo below.

Another alternative for the home is to get on the floor on your hands and knees. Grasp the weight in one hand and raise your arm behind you toward the ceiling as high as you can comfortably go. Hold for the count of three and repeat ten times. Alternate sides for up to three sets.

EXERCISES FOR THE UPPER ARM

The bicep curl — In the gym, this exercise can be done with a resistance machine or with free weights. While seated on a machine with your feet comfortably apart, rest your elbows on the shoulder-level pad and using an underhand

Bicep curl

grip, grasp the handles and pull them toward your shoulders. At home, using free weights, stand with your feet comfortably apart, grasp a dumbbell or small barbell in each hand. (Elbows should be slightly in front of and against your body, with the palms up for biceps.) Lift the weight. You can change to thumbs up or palms down to work the forearm.

The tricep extension — To use the resistance machine, sit with your feet comfortably apart and your back straight. Rest your elbows on the padded shelf, just below shoulder height. Grasp the bars and pull them down. At home while sitting with free weights, grasp a dumbbell or barbell with both hands and hold it behind your head (keep your hands close to your head, elbows pointing up). Begin the exercise with the weight hanging down behind your head and raise the weight by straightening your arms. Lower the weight carefully.

EXERCISES FOR THE LOWER ARM OR FOREARM

The wrist curl — In the gym or at home, using free weights, sit on a weight bench or chair. Hold the weight in your hand and lay the back of your arm down on your thigh (your arm must be flat on your thigh from the elbow to the wrist with the palm of your hand facing up). Allow your hand to drop down over the knee. Now, curl the hand up and lower it back down. Repeat with the other hand.

The wrist extension — Position your arm exactly as in the wrist curl, but your palm should face the floor. Raise and lower your hand.

EXERCISES FOR THE HIP, UPPER AND LOWER LEGS

The leg press — Using a resistance machine, begin with your knees near your chest. Push against the footrest. Do not completely straighten your legs. At home you can do modified squats with your back against the wall. Place your feet about twelve inches in front of you and about twelve inches apart and lower yourself, keeping your knees over your feet. You will end in a sitting position digging your heels into the floor, and then rise to your original position.

The quadriceps extension — In the gym, using the knee-extension machine, hook

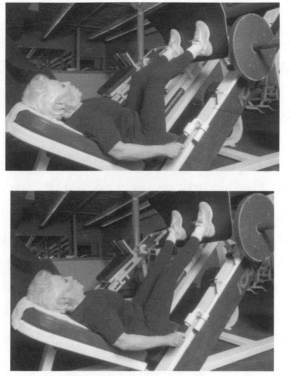

your feet behind the padded bar and lift
both feet at the same time, then slowly
lower the bar. At home, use Velcro ankle
weights. Sit in a chair with your back sup-
ported and extend your knee by raising
one leg at a time.

The calf raise — Using free weights, hold
one in each hand with your arms at your
sides, palms facing your sides. With your
feet six to eight inches apart, rise up on
your toes and lower yourself back down.

The shoulder shrug — Stand just as in the
calf raise. Do not rise up on your toes; instead, shrug your shoulders as high as you

can and then let them back down.

AEROBIC, WEIGHT-BEARING EXERCISE

Walking — Walk streets near your home, on tracks at schools and parks, in malls, or on city streets. You can walk anywhere as long as the surface is smooth, level, and stable. If walking does not appeal to you, pick another aerobic, weight-bearing ac-

tivity (or two or three) and make it part of a weekly routine.

2. Exercises for Women with Osteoporosis

Even if a woman already has osteoporosis, exercise is crucial to prevent further bone loss. In addition, exercise can reduce pain. However, no exercise routine for women with osteoporosis should be one that requires any of the following:

- Spine flexion — This means that the exercise should not require bending forward from the waist with the back rounded (e.g., old-fashioned sit-ups or toe-touches). No twisting of spine.
- Jarring the spine — This means no jumping, and no high-impact aerobics, jogging, or running.
- Anything that increases the risk for falling. No trampolines or step aerobics.
- Moving your legs sideways or across your body against resistance.

Start your program gradually in order to build endurance and avoid injury. This exercise program includes aerobic weight-bearing activity (walking); isotonic strength-training to target areas where fractures are most common and to improve coordination and balance; isometric abdominal exercises; and spine-extension exercises (not spine flexion).

AEROBIC WEIGHT-BEARING ACTIVITY

Regular walking program — Walking is crucial to prevent osteoporosis. Follow the earlier guidelines.

BACK-EXTENSION EXERCISES AND ISOMETRIC ABDOMINAL EXERCISES

The following exercises were designed specifically for women with osteoporosis by Dr. Mehrsheed Sinaki and her colleagues at the Mayo Clinic. Any woman with osteoporosis should check with her own doctor or physical therapist before attempting the following exercises.

The first two exercises are performed sitting in a chair. It is preferable if the chair has no sides or arms to get in the way.

1. Sit up straight with both feet comfortably on the floor. Raise your arms behind your head and place the fingertips of both hands against

the back of your head. Now, keeping your back straight and your chin level with the floor, slowly push your elbows back as far as they will go, leaving your fingers against the back of your head. Then allow your elbows to come forward gently. Repeat this up to fifteen times.

2. Stay seated in the chair and drop your arms down to your sides. Bend your arms at the elbow and keep your elbows against your sides. Now, sitting up straight, push both elbows behind your back, as though you were trying to touch your elbows together. Push them back gently, but as far as you can. Then let them come forward. Repeat this exercise ten to fifteen times.

3. Lie facedown on the floor. A pillow should be placed under your lower chest and abdomen or hips. Place your arms at your sides. Tuck your chin in and then lift your head up just far enough so that it is level with your shoulders. Then lower your head back to the floor. Do not attempt too many repetitions at first. Build up to ten or fifteen times.

4. Modified sit-ups. Lie faceup on the

floor with your knees bent at about a ninety-degree angle. Place your arms across your chest or abdomen. Tuck your chin and lift your head and shoulders up only far enough to get the tops of your shoulders off the floor. *Do not raise your head any*

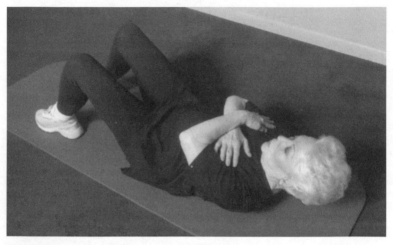

Modified sit-up

farther. Then lower your head back down. This modified sit-up can be repeated up to fifteen times.

5. Lie on a flat, firm surface, faceup. Place your hands under your hips. Do not raise your head during the exercise. Lift your feet off the floor about six inches, keeping your legs straight. Lower your feet to the floor and repeat ten times.

6. Half squat. You need to hold on to a

heavy piece of furniture or railing about waist high for this exercise. Stand with your feet comfortably apart, toes forward. While holding onto the object, lower your body by bending your knees about halfway down. Come back up and repeat fifteen times. Keep your back straight. This exercise can also be performed against a wall as in the leg-press-at-home section.

Each exercise set above should be done twice a day.

You can begin with one- to three-pound free weights, and perform the following exercises (for directions, see the exercises in the program for prevention of osteoporosis):

Bicep curl   Wrist curl   Wrist extension
Tricep extension   Shoulder shrug

Start with ten repetitions of each exercise. Build up to twenty-five repetitions. The weights can increase as you get stronger. These exercises can be done every other day, three days a week.

Everyday tricks for anyone to help strengthen

the muscles and prevent injury to bones:

- When getting out of a chair, move to the edge of the seat, keep your feet apart, one slightly in front of the other, and try to stand up straight without giving a little push on your thighs or the arm of the chair. This helps to strengthen thigh muscles and helps with balance.
- When walking up stairs, use the whole foot rather than your tiptoes.
- Keeping the spine straight (with ears over the shoulders) and walking with good posture protects the spine.
- Any object to be picked up from the floor should always be as close to you as possible, so drag it closer before picking it up. Then pick it up by squatting and bending the knees with feet apart for increased balance rather than using the back.
- When placing dishes in the dishwasher try not to bend the back. Squat instead.
- When taking clothes out of the dryer try not to bend from the waist. Instead, squat at the knees to remove the clothes.
- When changing sheets and placing

fitted corners, try using the leg muscles, not the back.

- When removing packages from the car, particularly from the trunk, drag the object as close to you as possible before attempting to lift it.
- When carrying groceries, divide the load equally in two bags and carry with elbows slightly bent at sides and with a straight head, neck, and back.

Fall Prevention

I broke my hand when I fell, and Mama fell in her apartment at the assisted living facility. Of otherwise healthy men and women over the age of sixty-five, 35–40 percent fall. No one gave me advice about reducing my risk of falling.

WHY DO WE FALL?

Many studies have been conducted to determine the major risk factors for falling, with a particular emphasis on finding those factors that can be eliminated or modified. Visual problems are a major cause of falls. This includes nearsightedness, farsightedness, cataracts, and macular degeneration.

Be sure to stay current on trips to the ophthalmologist and have adequate home lighting.

People also fall due to poor upper–leg muscle strength. These are the muscles that provide stability to the knees when we walk and sit down or stand up. If you have seen people who fall or drop into a chair it is because in all likelihood, their upper leg muscles are weak. Exercise will strengthen these muscles.

Poor balance is also a cause of accidental falls. There are several causes of poor bal-

Assess Your Balance

Doctors test balance with an exam called the Get Up and Go Test. You can try the test at home.

Get up from a chair without using your arms. Walk several steps. Turn around and walk back to the chair. Sit without using your arms. Simple, right? If you experience signs of imbalance, consult your doctor. He or she should perform a full evaluation of your balance.

ance. The measure of balance is called "body-sway." This refers to the ability to right the body or keep it straight when it is suddenly pushed sideways. Part of the ability to regain stability depends on the balance centers in the brain, but it also depends on the strength of your back and stomach muscles. These muscles can be strengthened through exercise. My trainers work with me regularly to improve my balance.

Inner-ear problems can be a source of poor balance. A condition called peripheral neuropathy can affect your ability to know if your feet are on the ground. Dizziness when standing is another hazard. Dizziness can occur because the body does not get the blood to the brain fast enough when standing or because the balance centers in the inner ear do not react properly to the change in positions.

Finally, there are medications that may increase the risk of falling because they interfere with alertness or balance. These are medications such as sedatives, tranquilizers, painkillers, and antidepressants. If this is the case, some medications might be changed. Be sure to talk to your doctor if you are having problems with balance or falling. The exercise programs outlined earlier will help improve coordination and balance and thus help to lower the risk of falling.

EXERCISES TO IMPROVE BALANCE

One-leg stand: I stand on one leg while holding weights.

Teeter board: I stand on the teeter board and toss a ball back and forth with my trainer. I also stand on inflated cushions while holding weights.

Trainers tell me that these exercises build memory in my ankles and improve my stability and my balance.

Tai chi has also been known to improve balance and reduce the risk of falling.

In addition to exercise, it is crucial that you fall-proof your home, office, or any other place where you spend time.

HOME FALL-PROOFING

Making a home fall-proof is essential. The following guidelines were created by the American Geriatrics Society in conjunction with the British Geriatric Society and the American Academy of Orthopedic Surgeons Panel on Fall Prevention.

- Area rugs on smooth floors or even on carpeted surfaces are hazardous. If you have area rugs, put a gripper pad or nonskid mat underneath.
- Handrails should be installed by any stairs or steps in the house or leading to the house from the outside.
- Good lighting is important throughout the house. An inexpensive automatic night-light will work. Light sensors are great for lighting outdoor stairwells at night.
- Slippery surfaces. These are obvious hazards but we do not always pay attention to them. Clean up spills immediately.
- Bathtubs and showers. Be careful if you use bath oil. Some of the newer tubs have been made with irregular surfaces to prevent slipping, but this improvement does not make the tub safe enough. A rubber bath mat or adhesive decals applied to the bottom of the tub will improve traction. When getting out of the tub, do not grab for the towel rack. Safety bars should be installed in showers and baths.
- Nighttime routes through the house should be clear. Most falls occur at

night when people get up to check on a child, or go to the bathroom or the kitchen. Examine the route and make sure that automatic night-lights illuminate this path. Before going to sleep, make sure there are no objects on the path that could cause a fall. Keep a flashlight next to the bed in case more light is needed.

- Kitchen cabinets should be organized so that climbing on stools and stepladders is not necessary.
- Electric cords should not lie in traffic areas.
- Stairs should be kept clear of any clutter.

WHAT YOU WEAR CAN MAKE A DIFFERENCE

Mama taught me that a woman is always supposed to look like a lady. She said that no self-respecting woman would ever have straight hair (she made this rule after home permanents came on the market); as a girl I learned never to wear white before Easter; when traveling, wear gloves; wear stockings and wear heels.

I have abandoned all ladylike pretensions. I do not own any shoes with heels higher than one inch, nor do I own a skirt. I dress for comfort and safety. Also, wearing comfortable shoes makes it easy to fit an exercise walk into a routine errand.

CLOTHING TIPS

Shoes — The best shoe is a low-heeled shoe with a square box toe. The shoe should have a shock-absorbing heel and a slip-resistant sole. The upper part of the shoe should be flexible or soft and the back should come up over the heel so the foot does not slip out of the shoe. Shoes designed for walking will have an outer sole and insole designed to support and cushion the foot as the heel strikes the ground and the shoe contacts the ground from heel to toe. Running shoes are designed to do the same, although they usually have even more shock absorption built into the heel because the impact is greater when the runner hits the ground. Running shoes work for walking, but other shoes do not. Tennis shoes are designed to support the foot during side-to-side movements of the toes. They are not designed for repetitive heel impacts and heel to toe movements. Cross trainers attempt to give a little bit of each. They are better than tennis shoes for walking, but not as good as walking or running shoes. Deck shoes intended for boats are not exercise shoes at all. Most athletic stores will help you choose the right shoe. Be careful about wearing slippers. Some shoes with rubber or composite foam soles will catch on carpet and cause you to trip. Beware.

Skirts — Tight skirts can make it difficult to walk. Make sure you can walk comfortably in any skirt, or better yet, wear pants.

Pants — Pants that are too long can cause you to trip. Make sure the pant leg is not long or wide enough to get underfoot.

I travel around the country to speak about women's health and specifically about osteoporosis. After I talk, women will come up to me and tell me how they wished their mothers could have heard me. And I always say, "Well, I am just glad that *you* heard me and I hope that you will get to a gym now." Some women say they will start next year or when they have more time. They say, "I will do it just as soon as X occurs." And of course X gets there and then, lo and behold, there is Y to keep them from taking care of themselves.

Women put restraints on their lives. They tell themselves they cannot go to the doctor or the gym, or take time to eat right because someone else is depending on them. Women carry guilt around by the bushel basket. The reality is that we hem ourselves in. I cannot do anything about the way women design their own shackles, but I can say with certainty that we must be self-sufficient so that we can go and do and experience wonderful new things. Stop using excuses for not taking care of yourself.

EPILOGUE

One of the messages I want passionately to spread about osteoporosis is that this is not an old person's disease — young people get it, too, and the younger years are when you build bone. Since doctors and researchers are making strides with the medicines that will keep women alive longer, all of us need to keep our bones healthy so those years can be vigorous ones.

A couple of years ago, I took a walking trip with my younger daughter, Ellen, from Florence to Siena. That is forty miles! We would start early in the morning, meet our guide, and walk through glorious fields of sunflowers. And then we would walk back to whatever town we were staying in, have lunch, and wander around cathedrals or shop. Afterward, we would dress for dinner, and then start over the next morning. I traveled to Machu Picchu in Peru with my daughter Cecile and some friends, where the terrain is rough and the ruins have old, primitive steps. My daughters gave me a raft trip down the Salt River in Arizona for one of my recent birthdays, and they still owe me a trip rafting the Grand Canyon. I have just returned from a trip to Kenya with a group of women. I turned sixty-nine in Africa and for my birthday I had a party that included Masai warriors dancing around the birthday table.

I love the time I spend traveling with my children and my friends. I remember when my first grandchild, Lily, was born. Cecile was in California and I went out to be with her. I had never thought about having grandchildren, but when I saw Lily, I felt the most incredible tenderness toward that child. My perspective was changed. I realized my life is going to go on in these little creatures that are born to my children. They are an extension of everything I am. Cecile says she is just a vehicle to bring Lily and me together.

I had promised Lily that when she was ten I would take her to London. Right before we left, it dawned on me that the queen might see us, since she had come to Texas to visit us. I sent a fax to Buckingham Palace saying that I was bringing my granddaughter to London. I was sure the queen would remember her because Lily had given her a bouquet of posies.

I got a fax back right away saying to come the following Tuesday at 11:45. I had no idea that this was right in the middle of the changing of the guard. There were thousands of people to see the changing of the guard at Buckingham Palace and Lily, Cecile, and I marched right through the gate. We visited the queen in the family quarters and she was very sweet to Lily. We had tea and they chatted about the things we should do while we were in London.

Queen Elizabeth had arranged for one of the ladies in waiting to take us on a tour of the palace. When we left, we walked across the gravel yard in front of the palace. I thought, Here we are so high on the hog, it just does not get any better than this. I asked Lily what she would remember about the day and Lily said, "The queen had lipstick on her teeth."

Isn't that wonderful? Children keep things in perspective for us. I have enjoyed every stage of my life, but I particularly love this one. I have the most independence I have ever enjoyed and the most wisdom. I have lived through enough to know what living is about and I have made peace with who I am. I have learned what gives me pleasure and that it is OK to have fun. I owe most of it to my health. The greatest gift you can give to your children and the people you love is your own good health.

TYPICAL QUESTIONS

1. *My back hurts. Should I worry that I have osteoporosis? What symptoms will I have that indicate I am developing osteoporosis?*

There are many reasons for back pain. Osteoporosis is one possibility, but the disease does not usually cause physical pain unless there is a fracture. Talk to a physician to figure out if a fracture is causing the pain (which can be determined by an X ray), or if there is another source, unrelated to osteoporosis. Unless a bone is broken or bone density is measured, it is difficult or impossible to know when bone mass is deteriorating because there are virtually no physical symptoms.

2. *Who gets osteoporosis most often?*

Women are by far the majority of those who suffer from osteoporosis for a variety of reasons, including bone loss as a result of menopause, less physical activity as children, and lower calcium consumption. But men can — and do — still develop osteoporosis.

3. *Why should we worry about osteoporosis if we are going to get it when we grow older anyway?*

Osteoporosis is not a condition that happens simply because of age. It is a disease that can be prevented. If we take the proper steps throughout our lives to ensure that we get enough calcium, and build up our bone mass through exercise, we will not necessarily get osteoporosis when we grow older.

4. *Both my mother and grandmother shrunk as they got older. My mother lost a total of five inches. Is their shrinking a cause of osteoporosis?*

Brittle, osteoporotic bones in the spine often fracture or collapse easily, causing permanent loss of height, so their loss of height could be due to osteoporosis.

5. *What can I do if I already have osteoporosis?*

A combination of medication, calcium and vitamin D intake, and exercise can prevent future bone loss and ease the pain of existing fractures. The FDA has approved Evista, Fosamax, Actonel, Calcimar, Miacalcin, and Forteo for the treatment of osteoporosis, and these medications may help to slow bone loss and reduce the risk of fractures.

6. *Are there other things I can do for my bones rather than take drugs?*

The recommendations made in this book are based on traditional medicine with an emphasis on lifestyle issues, rather than natural or alternative medicine. There is a body of information on alternative medicine you may want to explore on your own.

7. *Is osteoporosis a genetic disorder?*

The amount of bone a person builds up in his or her youth seems to be determined at least in part by genetics, which affects the likelihood of developing osteoporosis later in life. However, the amount of bone lost during adulthood may be related to genetics as well as other factors.

8. *What is the difference between osteoarthritis and osteoporosis?*

In osteoarthritis, the lining of the joints becomes inflamed, which is usually painful and can eventually destroy the joint. Osteoporosis affects the bone itself, leaving it weak and brittle as it loses minerals and mass. Someone could be diagnosed with both osteoarthritis and osteoporosis.

9. *What do I need to know about calcium supplements?*

Ideally, calcium should be obtained from diet rather than supplements. But it is very difficult to get enough calcium from diet alone and the most important thing is to get plenty of it, whether from diet or a supplement (see Chapter 7). When taking supplements, read the label carefully and use the amounts of calcium recommended by either the NIH or the National Academy of Science. (It is possible to get too much calcium. The kidneys cannot remove more than 3,000–4,000mg a day.) It is preferable to get calcium throughout the day rather than all at once, but again, be sure to read the label on your supplements. Some types are best taken with food while others are more beneficial when taken on an empty stomach. Most people do not suffer any side effects from calcium supplements, but some, particularly calcium carbonate supplements, can cause constipation and gas.

10. *My mother is in her eighties and the new doctor she is seeing has just advised her to start taking calcium. Isn't it too late?*

No. It is never too late to benefit from calcium, though it provides different benefits for different age groups. In the older population, calcium can help stop bone loss and perhaps even reduce the risk of hip fractures (see Chapter 7).

11. *I have been told by a friend that I must take a vitamin D supplement along with calcium. Is this true?*

Yes and no. Vitamin D helps the body properly absorb calcium, but because it is available simply from exposure to the sun, most people under age sixty do not need extra vitamin D (unless they do not get any sun exposure). After age sixty, however, it is good to get additional vitamin D. It does not need to be taken at the same time as the calcium — in fact, any vitamin D taken today will help the body absorb calcium tomorrow.

12. Is taking magnesium important?

Magnesium, like calcium, is a mineral, but our bodies really do not need very much of it. What little we do need is easily available in most people's diets, unless a person is taking a diuretic, in which case the body can lose magnesium. If taking diuretics, consult a doctor about getting enough magnesium.

13. How does smoking affect the risk of osteoporosis?

Smoking increases the risk of osteoporosis because it changes estrogen in the liver so that it does not protect the bones as well. Menopause also comes earlier to women who smoke, thereby speeding up the bone loss that accompanies it.

14. Can I drink coffee regularly and not compromise my bones?

Caffeine is a problem because it causes

the body to lose calcium (see Chapter 6 for sources of caffeine). In order to avoid this problem, try not to drink more than two caffeinated beverages per day.

15. *Are there medications that cause osteoporosis?*

Yes. Some medications, while often vital for the treatment of other problems, can cause bone mass to deteriorate, resulting in osteoporosis (see the list of these medications in Chapter 4). If you are taking a medication that may cause bone loss, talk to your doctor about ways to counteract this problem, but do not stop taking these medications on your own.

16. *When can I expect menopause to begin?*

The average age of menopause is fifty to fifty-one. When you start to become menopausal, your periods will become irregular and you might experience hot flashes.

17. *I am not a great fan of exercise. What workout can I do that is efficient and offers protection for my bones?*

Weight-bearing, strength-training exercises and walking are the best types of exercise to protect bones, though you must walk at least three miles (preferably four miles) a few times a week. Although swimming and bicycling are great aerobic exercises, they are not good bone protectors.

18. *Is there a test that can tell me if I am at risk of developing osteoporosis?*

A bone-density test.

19. *Which bone-density test should I have?*

There are a few different bone-density tests (see Chapter 3) that can be performed on different places of the body. Talk to your doctor about your options, but be aware that different doctors have different opinions on this subject. I recommend scanning the spine and hip.

20. *How dangerous is the amount of radiation I will receive from a bone-density test?*

The amount of radiation an individual will receive is minimal. Radiation from bone-density tests like DEXA is nothing to worry about.

21. *How often do I need a bone-density test?*

If a woman does not have osteoporosis, she needs to have a bone-density test two or three times during her life. Many doctors recommend that a bone-density test be given between age fifty and sixty, but it is never too late. For individuals whose bone-density levels are normal, the test should be done every five years. However, for individuals with osteoporosis or low bone mass, a test every one or two years will help monitor the progress of treatment.

22. *I am a model of the woman who should not have to worry about osteoporosis. I do not smoke or drink. I am careful to get sufficient calcium. I exercise regularly. There is also no osteoporosis in my family. I assume I need not worry about osteoporosis when I am in menopause.*

All of these positive habits and circumstances will be beneficial, but calcium and exercise are not always enough to protect the bones through menopause. A bone-density test will help determine whether the bones are healthy.

23. *How can I help my mother who has osteoporosis and is in pain?*

There are a few treatments available. Salmon calcitonin is one option. There are also procedures called vertebroplasty and kyphoplasty that inject a substance into the vertebrae and can reduce pain and strengthen bone. Finally, it may help to formulate an exercise program with a doctor.

24. *Can estrogen be taken in combination with the other medications available to treat osteoporosis?*

Yes. Recent studies have confirmed that combining estrogen with one of the bisphosphonate medicines does increase bone density better than either drug alone. But the changes in the risk for fracture due to these combinations have not been tested. Combining treatments also seems to be perfectly safe, but talk to your doctor before doing so.

25. *Is the "dowager's hump" an inevitable sign of growing older?*

No. It is caused by multiple fractures of vertebrae that change the curve of the spine and cause the individual to stand in a position that makes the spine look humped. This is a direct result of osteoporosis.

RESOURCES

National Osteoporosis Foundation
1232 22nd Street, N.W.
Washington, DC 20037
Phone: 202-223-2226
Web site: *www.nof.org*

National Institutes of Health Osteoporosis and Related Bone Diseases National Resource Center
1232 22nd Street, N.W.
Washington, DC 20037
Phone: 800-624-BONE or 202-223-0344
Fax: 202-293-2356
Web site: *www.osteo.org*
E-mail: *orbdnrc@nof.org*

North American Menopause Society
PO Box 94527
Cleveland, OH 44101
Automated Information Line:
    800-774-5342
Telephone: 440-442-7550

Fax: 440-442-2660
Web site: *www.menopause.org*
E-mail: *info@menopause.org*

American College of Obstetricians and Gynecologists
409 12th Street, S.W.
Washington, DC 20090
Phone: 202-638-5577
Web site: *www.acog.com*

National Dairy Council
c/o Dairy Management, Inc.
10255 W. Higgins Rd.
Suite 900
Rosemont, IL 60018
Phone: 800-853-2479 or 847-803-2000
Web site: *www.dairyinfo.com*
E-mail: *ndc@dairyinformation.com*

The Arthritis Foundation
PO Box 7669
Atlanta, GA 30357-0669
Phone: 800-283-7800
Web site: *www.arthritis.org*

American Academy of Orthopedic Surgeons
6300 N. River Rd.
Rosemont, IL 60018
Web site: *www.aaos.org*

Office of Minority Health Resource Center
PO Box 37337
Washington, DC 20013
Telephone: 800-444-6472
Fax: 301-589-0884
Web site: *www.omhrc.gov*
E-mail: *info@omhrc.gov*

Web sites

Foundation for Osteoporosis Research and Education
www.fore.org

National Women's Health Information Center
www.4woman.org

National Women's Health Resource Center
www.healthywomen.org

Local Osteoporosis Education Link
www.loel.net

Bone Measurement Institute (non-profit arm of Merck & Co., Inc.)
www.bonemeasurement.com

Menopause Online (sponsored by the Women's Health Center)
www.menopause-online.com

WebMD
www.webmd.com

Physicians Desk Reference
www.pdr.net

Doctor's Guide to the Internet
www.pslgroup.com

U.S. Food and Drug Administration Center for Food Safety and Applied Nutrition
www.cfsan.fda.gov

Food and Nutrition Information Center (sponsored by the U.S. Department of Agriculture)
www.nal.usda.gov/fnic

Nutrition Navigator (sponsored by Tufts University)
www.navigator.tufts.edu

ABOUT THE AUTHORS

Ann Richards was governor of Texas from 1990 to 1994, and has been active in politics for over half a century. In 1988, she gained national prominence with her keynote address at the Democratic National Convention. She divides her time between Texas and New York City.

Richard U. Levine, M.D., is a clinical professor of Obstetrics and Gynecology at the College of Physicians and Surgeons of Columbia University, and attending physician at the New York Presbyterian Hospital, where he serves as vice-chairman in the department of Obstetrics and Gynecology.

The employees of Thorndike Press hope you have enjoyed this Large Print book. All our Thorndike and Wheeler Large Print titles are designed for easy reading, and all our books are made to last. Other Thorndike Press Large Print books are available at your library, through selected bookstores, or directly from us.

For information about titles, please call:

(800) 223-1244

or visit our Web site at:

www.gale.com/thorndike
www.gale.com/wheeler

To share your comments, please write:

Publisher
Thorndike Press
295 Kennedy Memorial Drive
Waterville, ME   04901